John Brown

Also from Westphalia Press
westphaliapress.org

The Idea of the Digital University

Dialogue in the Roman-Greco World

The History of Photography

International or Local Ownership?: Security Sector Development in Post-Independent Kosovo

Lankes, His Woodcut Bookplates

Opportunity and Horatio Alger

The Role of Theory in Policy Analysis

The Little Confectioner

Non Profit Organizations and Disaster

The Idea of Neoliberalism: The Emperor Has Threadbare Contemporary Clothes

Social Satire and the Modern Novel

Ukraine vs. Russia: Revolution, Democracy and War: Selected Articles and Blogs, 2010-2016

James Martineau and Rebuilding Theology

A Strategy for Implementing the Reconciliation Process

Issues in Maritime Cyber Security

Understanding Art

Homeopathy

Fishing the Florida Keys

Iran: Who Is Really In Charge?

Contracting, Logistics, Reverse Logistics: The Project, Program and Portfolio Approach

The Thomas Starr King Dispute

Springfield: The Novel

Lariats and Lassos

Mr. Garfield of Ohio

The French Foreign Legion

War in Syria

Ongoing Issues in Georgian Policy and Public Administration

Growing Inequality: Bridging Complex Systems, Population Health and Health Disparities

Designing, Adapting, Strategizing in Online Education

Gunboat and Gun-runner

Pacific Hurtgen: The American Army in Northern Luzon, 1945

Natural Gas as an Instrument of Russian State Power

New Frontiers in Criminology

Feeding the Global South

John Brown

An Essay by
Hermann Von Holst

---

by Dr. Hermann Von Holst
Edited by Frank Preston Stearns

WESTPHALIA PRESS
An Imprint of Policy Studies Organization

John Brown: An Essay by Hermann Von Holst
All Rights Reserved © 2017 by Policy Studies Organization

Westphalia Press
An imprint of Policy Studies Organization
1527 New Hampshire Ave., NW
Washington, D.C. 20036
info@ipsonet.org

ISBN-13: 978-1-63391-617-3
ISBN-10: 1-63391-617-0

Cover design by Jeffrey Barnes:
jbarnesbook.design

Daniel Gutierrez-Sandoval, Executive Director
PSO and Westphalia Press

Updated material and comments on this edition
can be found at the Westphalia Press website:
www.westphaliapress.org

JOHN BROWN,

AN ESSAY BY HERMANN VON HOLST.

JOHN BROWN.

BY

DR. HERMANN VON HOLST,
PROFESSOR AT THE UNIVERSITY OF FREIBURG, IN BADEN.

EDITED BY

FRANK PRESTON STEARNS.

BOSTON
CUPPLES AND HURD, PUBLISHERS
The Algonquin Press

Copyright, *1888*,
BY CUPPLES AND HURD.

All rights reserved.

SECOND EDITION.

When souls reach a certain clearness of perception, they accept a knowledge and motive above selfishness. A breath of will blows eternally through the universe of souls in the direction of the Right and Necessary. It is the air which all intellects inhale and exhale, and it is the wind which blows the world into order and orbit.— *R. W. Emerson.*

Alas for the man who knows no "higher law," who holds himself in such absolute obedience to any power of governor or government on earth that he is not ready to listen when the demands of his own character say to him "disobey!" Alas for the man who thinks even the facts of Nature his inevitable masters, who will not believe in his power to overcome them, even though it be by undergoing them, who will not rush through fire, though it burn, through water, though it drown, to do the work which his soul knows that it must do! — *Phillips Brooks.*

PREFACE.

THE late attacks upon the memory of John Brown having aroused me to a sense of the danger which might result from them, — a danger not only to that hero but to all heroism in the future, — I looked about for some means by which their baneful influence might be counteracted. Fortunately I found close at hand an honest and sympathetic account of him by a German writer who has within the last few years achieved the highest rank as an authority on American history, recognized alike by liberal and conservative as an impartial judge of our public affairs. Not being in sufficiently good health to make a translation of this myself, I obtained the assistance for that purpose of Mr. Philippe Marcou, — an excellent philologist of Cambridge; and I believe that his version of Professor von Holst's essay will be found as nearly literal and accurate as is possible, considering the differences of idiom between the two languages. It is not always possible to render Von Holst's vigorous and comprehensive sentences into smoothly flowing English, and if the translator has anywhere sacrificed an elegant diction in order to reproduce the full sense of the original, the reader will doubtless decide that he has done rightly.

Such a writer is no creature of a day; and I have no fear but that his opinion of John Brown's life and death will be the one which future generations of Americans will accept. No rude hand will ever again reach high enough to pull down this record of his fame. The hostile shafts of the so-called realist will do him as little harm as the malign sympathy of the anarchist, or the indifference of the historical pedant.

The essay, however, is so closely connected with Von Holst's great work on the political and constitutional history of our country that I considered it advisable to prepare an introduction to it, in which to give some brief account of that history and the mental attitude of

Préface.

the writer toward it. This is not so much an abstract of the book (which would have been too difficult an undertaking for me), as a compendium of my own impressions after reading it. I felt that before considering John Brown himself some statement was required of the social and ethical problem which he undertook to solve, and through an understanding of which we find, in turn, the solution of his own character.

At the suggestion of my friends, I have published in an appendix a vindication of the character of John Brown from the principal charges which have within the last few years been brought against him, as well as some remarks on the bust of him by Brackett, from which the frontispiece in this volume is taken, and the account of a visit to the grave of John Brown, written by a distinguished member of the medical profession.

THE EDITOR.

CONTENTS.

	PAGE
INTRODUCTION	11
JOHN BROWN. AN ESSAY BY HERMANN VON HOLST	55
THE FLOODS. BY D. A. WASSON	179
APPENDIX.	
REMARKS ON THE JOHN BROWN BUST	185
REMARKS ON THE JOHN BROWN MEDAL	189
A VISIT TO THE GRAVE OF JOHN BROWN	197
UNFRIENDLY CRITICISM OF JOHN BROWN	204

INTRODUCTION.

INTRODUCTION.

HISTORIANS may be divided into three classes. Firstly is the rhetorical school, represented by Macaulay and Bancroft, who aim at producing a striking impression; secondly, there is the artistic school, to which Voltaire and Carlyle belong, — writers of great dramatic effect; and finally, — what may be called the scientific school, — those historians who only attempt to tell the plain facts in the simplest way, and give whatever explanation for them seems most probable. The difference between the first and the second is like the difference between the play-writer and the dramatic poet; the difference between the second and third is like that between the stage and the court-room. Of the latter class there has been during the present century no more conspicuous example than Dr. Hermann von Holst, professor of constitutional history in the University of Freiburg in Baden, Germany, or, as it is sometimes called, Freiburg in the Black Forest.

In one sense Americans are the most cosmopolitan of people, — for they travel everywhere and make themselves at home wherever they go. On the other hand Frenchmen travel but little, and the English commonly carry their island about with them, as a tortoise carries his shell on his back. But in another sense the Germans are the most cosmopolitan people, because they are the only people who take pains to obtain a clear and unprejudiced knowledge of other nations. The Prussian staff in 1870 knew more about the military condition of France than did

Napoleon III., or probably any one of his subordinates. German newspapers are much better judges of English politics than French or American papers are, and predict more correctly in regard to Oriental politics than the English press is able to. When Garfield was assassinated, the "Berlin Post" said, "His life is a sacrifice to the cause of good government;" and this was the only gleam of light which came to us from Europe in that dark period. When Alaska was purchased from Russia, a book on that country was immediately published in Germany from which one might suppose that the author had been studying the subject all his life, so thorough and exhaustive was it. About the time that Sainte-Beuve had concluded that German literature was coming to an end, Von Ranke was writing his "History of the Popes," and Mommsen preparing for his "History of Rome," both unsurpassed in their way. In the last century, Lessing and Goethe set such a bright example of high-minded impartiality in literature that their country-men could not but follow in the same path. As a sort of natural reaction, one sometimes meets with individual Germans who are the most bigoted and provincial of men, unwilling to discover virtue or excellence in any country or time but their own; but these do not represent cultivated Germany. Professor von Holst represents it a great deal better. In his great work called, "The Constitution and Democracy of the United States of America,"[1] he has given us a history so sympathetic and yet so impartial, so clear and yet so profound, so painstaking and accurate in details, and yet of such broad vision and correctness of logic, as probably no citizen of one nation has ever before writ-

[1] Verfassung und Demokratie der Verein-Staaten von Amerika. Von Dr. H. von Holst, Düsseldorf.

ten of another. Other European books on America, French and English, have a certain strangeness about them, — we read them as if we were reading of a foreign country, — but H. von Holst is native to the soil. He is at the same time friendly and inexorably just. He does not even suffer from that bias of impartiality which tries to balance opposing elements too nicely and produces an effect of indifference or indecision. He is a disinterested spectator, but by no means a cold one. Not too easily do we discover the character of the writer in his work; but at length it shines clearly forth from the pages, — his sincerity, his earnestness, his love of simplicity, his determination to bring order and truth out of the confusion and mendacity of party politics; above all, his respect for virtue, admiration of true greatness, and contempt for inflated pretension. We feel no little sympathy for him when we consider what a multitude of speeches he has been obliged to read, what long files of newspapers to hunt through, besides pamphlets, legal evidence, and other stuff, all in a language foreign to him; a sort of work which is like weeding a flower-garden where the weeds are large and numerous, and the flowers small and far between. Most notable is the respect in which he is held by the legal profession of our country.

A man of keen moral sense, even if narrow-minded, will usually be found on the right side of any public question. A broader mind which sees both sides pretty clearly often becomes indecisive on that account; while the man of full mental breadth who perfectly comprehends his subject is naturally a partisan of whichever side has a better show of justice than the other. Thus we find Von Holst in the five volumes of his history which have thus far been published in full sympathy with the anti-slavery movement, which he finds to have been the main element in our political evolution. At the same time he fully appreciates the position of the South. As Sumner said, when one of his friends pronounced a curse on Preston S. Brooks,—"You must not blame him, but slavery; he was the result of the institution,"— so Von Holst shows true human sympathy for a community doomed by the greed of the English commercial class to run through a course of Tartarean horrors. The forced importation of negroes into the colonies led inexorably to the horrors and desolation of a gigantic war. There was no help for it; individuals could have acted differently, but a community is in the hands of fate. Democracy and slavery in the same government were like a lion and a bear in the same cage; both are compelled to fight for self-preservation.

For the Northern States to rid themselves of this curse was not difficult, — for their economical conditions were not favorable to it; but in the Southern States it flourished as monstrous things only can in a hot climate. It became the mainspring of the Southerner's life. It ruled all his actions and drove him forward in a course from which he could not turn. It filled his pockets, and made life comfortable for him. It gave its own tone to his thought, and its color to his actions. It produced a rapid and superficial civilization which is similar to the strength given by successive doses of opium, — the more we take of it the more we have to, until we reach moral and physical bankruptcy. When finally it became a political lever, the evil increased in geometrical ratio.

What made American slavery worse than any previous form of it, was that in a democracy the individual has more free-

Introduction. 19

dom and is more irresponsible than under other forms of government. This permitted every Southern planter to be an autocrat on his own estate, with the possibility always of his becoming a sort of Nero. The central government could pass no laws regulating slavery outside of the District of Columbia, nor could the President of the United States protect the negro from the fury of his master. The governments of the Southern States were in the hands of the slave-holders (Von Holst calls them the slavocracy), who naturally moulded the State laws in the interests of their class. Every planter was more than a king, for he could put his black subjects to death without even the form of a court-martial. I have never heard nor read that any American slave-owner was brought to justice for maltreatment of his slaves. There was virtually no law which regulated the relation between master and slave; whereas the Emperor Claudius enacted that any slave exposed by his master during sickness should be considered free, and under the Antonines the power of a Roman citizen to put his slaves to death was abolished altogether. In Athens also, slave-murder was held to be a crime sometimes punishable with death. The serfdom of the Middle Ages can only be compared to American slavery as claret may be compared to brandy. The serfs were only serfs with respect to their seigneurs; by all other persons they were to be treated like freemen. They could sue in the courts and obtain justice, such as it was in those days, and in extreme cases of ill-treatment even against the seigneur himself. They were attached to the land, and their ownership could rarely be transferred without it. Manumission was frequent, both for industry and bravery. Runaway serfs who escaped to a free city could not be reclaimed after the expiration of a certain time. The Catholic Church, in those days a pure fount of mercy, made constant efforts to ameliorate their condition, and at length obtained their total emancipation; whereas in America the Catholic clergy always supported the pro-slavery ticket in politics, and the whole Christian Church in the Southern States was a strong prop to the peculiar institutions there.

Perhaps a well-regulated serfdom for one or two generations would have been the best arrangement for the raw material when first imported from Africa. It would have served as the negro's apprenticeship to civilization and trained him up in good and useful ways. We all go through this discipline as children, and why not also the great child of the tropics? — the equatorial grasshopper, as Theodore Parker called him. But it is not in this way that human institutions are formed. Passion and superstition unbalance their judgment; the pendulum swings ever from side to side. We have first the Carolina slave code, and within a few days Governor Moses and universal negro suffrage. The theory that white slavery was wrong, but black slavery right, was a kind of bad logic with which people stilled their consciences for two hundred years, until at last the recoil set in. It came to be seen more and more certainly that the negro belonged to the great human brotherhood, and though there was a difference between a Zulu and a Saxon, that it was not like the difference between a man and a dog. Even in Jefferson's time the Virginia negro had become a fairly intelligent personage. Hamilton proposed to make soldiers of them and give them their freedom in return for fighting the British,— a feasible plan, as has since been proven. After the two races had become a good deal mixed, and a great many slaves were to be found who owned a quarter or only an eighth of negro descent, it required a still more forcible perversion of honest reasoning to believe that all these were doomed by the curse upon Ham. It was fairly sitting upon the safety-valve of one's conscience. A new and most dangerous element was now introduced into the problem; namely, the superior intelligence of these comparatively white negroes. Instead of encouraging this, laws were passed for the purpose of repressing it. Among Roman slaves mental ability was the common passport to emancipation; but in our Southern States it was more likely to lead to suspicion, harsh treatment, and ultimate ruin. Von Holst mentions the slave code of Maryland as a most disgraceful collection of legal enactments; and the pro-slavery Constitution which Missourians attempted to force upon

Kansas would have done little discredit to the Spanish Inquisition.

That in drafting the Constitution, slaves should have been spoken of as "persons held to labor" is curious enough; but what would some Italian or Hungarian lawyer who only knew of America as a place of immigration make out of such a clause as this: The first clause of Section Nine, Article First says, —

"The migration or importation of such persons as any of the States now existing shall think proper to admit, shall not be prohibited by Congress prior to the year one thousand eight hundred and eight; but a tax or duty may be imposed on such importation, not exceeding ten dollars for each person."

What American boy who now learns the Constitution of his country in the public schools could guess of his own wits what this was intended for? I was formerly

Introduction. 25

myself indebted to Justice Story for an explanation of it. He says, " This clause, as is manifest from its language, was designed solely to reserve to the Southern States for a limited period the right to import slaves." I do not think this is manifest from its language. It is only manifest by proving a negative; manifest, because at that time the clause could not refer to anything else. It could be applied equally well now to the importation under contract of free Croats or Italians to labor at a specified price. Why, therefore, this ambiguity? Why not call a slave a slave, as well as a spade a spade? In a national constitution, if anywhere, language should be clear, explicit, and unmistakable. Did then the wise framers of our government make use of such terms in deference to popular prejudices? Was it in deference to the prejudices of the North, or to the prejudices of the South? Sumner said that it was because our noble ancestors were unwilling to have the Constitution appear to support slavery or for the national government to recognize slavery, and brings good evidence to support his plea. Is it not also an evidence of shame, a consciousness of wrong, acquiesced in also by the representatives of slave-holding States? We may infer this from Jefferson's celebrated utterance on the subject, "Indeed, I tremble for my country when I reflect that God is just." Thus, from the cradle was our nation possessed of a guilty conscience which became intensified with time, but which developed itself very differently in the two opposing sections. In the Northern States it produced an ever increasing disgust of negro slavery and a sort of religious belief that it was a curse upon the national life, and contrary to divine law,—a belief inevitably tending to fanaticism in ardent and impulsive natures. In

Introduction. 27

the Southern States it led more and more to an attempt at self-justification by specious and sophistical reasoning, thus subverting man's moral consciousness and resulting in that ugliest type of fanaticism which is evolved from the worship of false idols. Calhoun, as Von Holst mentions, proved himself a true prophet when he warned his constituents that the greatest danger to slavery would arise from the instruction in Northern pulpits and school-houses; but he neglected to warn them that no less a danger lay concealed in the influence of their institutions upon themselves, especially from the effort to justify what could never be morally justified. Nothing is more pernicious either for an individual or a community than the constant habit of self-justification. It subverts the conscience, undermines character, and leads from self-deception to self-delusion, and that infatuation which, as Æschylus says, "has death for its fruits." The wise way for the slave-holders would have been to have avoided agitation, and in regard to slavery to have rested their defence upon a legal basis only. There were some who perceived this and acted accordingly, but the great majority proved the truth of Hamilton's maxim[1] that man is more a reasoning than a reasonable animal. What to them was the outcry of the Abolitionists, a handful of unknown people without position or influence? Yet from the first day they were enraged to fury by the accusation that slavery was wrong. It was the still small voice — as Phillips afterwards said, "it was the John Brown in every man's conscience" — which so alarmed them.

The Southerners, however, are not to be blamed for the results of slavery, even for its influence upon themselves, except so

[1] Alexander Hamilton, and not the English metaphysician, who was perhaps an illustration of it.

far as all of us are to blame for shirking the plain obligations of the golden rule. As long as cotton was king in the republic, it is not likely that a co-operative movement for gradual emancipation would have been successful. The tares were so imbedded with the wheat that one could not be eradicated without pulling up the other. Calhoun was also quite right when he declared that the interests of the slave-holders could not be trusted to legislators who were not slave-holders, and that therefore the South must acquire new territory and new States to balance the rapidly increasing population of the North. It must maintain a supremacy in the Union if it was to remain part of the Union. That supremacy once gone, slavery would go with it, for an equality with free labor was not possible. The best argument for a protective tariff is that it creates a diversity of material interests. It is unfortunate for any country when one particular interest in it predominates over all others, as the commercial interest in England, which has so often disturbed its relations with semi-civilized nations, and so also the offspring of its cupidity, African slavery in the United States. The slave-holders as a class are not therefore to be blamed, — for they were only puppets in the hands of fate; but those Southern politicians who in disregard of the prophetic warnings of Calhoun stirred up sectional hatred among the masses so as to advance their own personal ends, — those Southern Congressmen who persuaded their ignorant constituencies that the population of the free States were mean-spirited, cowardly wretches, "mudsills," scarcely better than vermin, — for them what condemnation can be too severe? The coarsest arts of the demagogue were made use of to intensify provincial prejudices, and after a time it happened that the caucus orator who was able to vilify the Northern people in the most extravagant language (like the Louisiana representative mentioned by Webster in his oration of the seventh of March), was the one surest to gain an election. There were many in the Northern States also who were unable to distinguish between the wickedness of the institution and the innocence of those to whom it was an inheritance. There were some among the Abolitionists who considered it a stain upon the pure character of Washington himself that he had been a slave-holder. The anti-slavery people who would not vote for Henry Clay in 1844 because he was a slave-holder threw away the last chance of preventing the annexation of Texas and the extension of slavery in that direction. Wendell Phillips afterward accused Webster and Clay of promoting the Mexican War; whereas they were both as much opposed to it as he was. Men of this class were, however, sincere and free from personal ambition, for the road to public offices lay in the opposite direction.

The influence of slavery on American political life is made beautifully clear by Von Holst in his minute painstaking manner. What he has not yet referred to, if I remember rightly, is its effect in determining the Southern character. The slaveholders, especially Virginians, possessed indeed, some virtues which enabled them to appear to Europeans in favorable contrast with other Americans. Plantation life with its tendency to indolence and prodigality, also developed rare courage, self-reliance, and a cheerful hospitality. No army ever endured privations with less complaint or fought more heroically in a good cause than General Lee's army in a bad one. From the soldier's point of view it was not a bad cause. So after the war an equal heroism was shown by great numbers of Southern ladies, who, educated in extreme luxury, but now widowed, orphaned, their property gone, cheerfully set themselves to earn their own livelihood in whatever honest way lay open to them. Nevertheless, Southern culture before the war was not in harmony with the spirit of our times. Jefferson has referred to that brutality which was the moral reaction of slavery upon the master; but the possession of unlimited power over men, and especially over women, engenders an equally pernicious and almost insane arrogance. Abundant instances of this are to be found in the Congressional debates of thirty years ago, and in Southern newspapers of the same period. Mommsen seems to have been the first, perhaps the only European who has appreciated this fact, although there is a hint of it in Thackeray's last novel. This only can explain the fatal self-confidence with which the slavocracy challenged to war the greatly superior power of the free States, seven millions against twenty, thus verifying the old adage of a haughty spirit to a degree never before known. By their own violence and temerity the slave-holders accomplished a revolution which might otherwise have been deferred a hundred years. Stephens of Georgia recognized the fact afterward when he denominated secession as a gigantic blunder. There was no expectation of immediate, scarcely of remote, emancipation among the masses who first voted for Lincoln. In 1857 Mommsen wrote, "When once the slave-holding aristocracy of Virginia and the Carolinas shall have carried matters as far as their congeners in the Sullan Rome, Cæsarism will there too be legitimized in the view of the spirit of history;"[1] and in another passage, "All the arrant sins that

[1] History of Rome, bk. v. ch. xi.

Introduction. 35

capital has been guilty of in the modern world against nationality and civilization, remain as far inferior to the abominations of the ancient capitalist States as the freeman, be he ever so poor, remains superior to the slave; and not until the dragon-seed of North America ripens, will the world have similar fruits to reap."

De Tocqueville in his bright but superficial book on democracy in America declines altogether to grapple with Southern society and the slavery question; yet that was democratic also in its political machinery, and the most important factor in the whole problem. Von Holst, however, is no compromiser, but seizes boldly upon his subject. He finds slavery in a democratic republic to be such a political inconsistency as could only end in violent revolution; and Thucydides never made a better statement. Thomas Jefferson represented in his own life these two contradictory sides, for he was the first notable antislavery writer as well as the author of the Southern gospel of secession, — the Kentucky and Virginia Resolutions, which have become so famous. He was at once a romantic political theorist and the most skilful of party politicians. He drafted the Declaration of Independence; but state rights, the election of judges by ballot, the substitution of metaphysical formulas for true political consideration, even the use of slander as a party weapon, may be said to have originated with him also. Being anchored to nothing firm or durable, he floated with the current of his time, and sympathized with every popular movement,[1] good or bad. What has been called his happy optimism was his happy unconsciousness of this self-contradiction.

The seed sown in Jefferson's time sprang

[1] The abolition of slavery was not a popular movement in Virginia, but it was so in France.

Introduction. 37

up in Jackson's, — debasement of the civil service; monstrous defalcations; shameful violation of treaties and constitutional rights; and finally, nullification. It is in his perfect comprehension of Jackson and his times that Von Holst shows himself the great historian. The Seminole War originated through slavery and consequently made thousands of Abolitionists in the free States. Inexorably as truth itself Von Holst traces, on one hand, the more and more fruitless efforts at compromise between slavery and free labor, and on the other, those dark conspiracies and fraudulent acts by which the slavocracy frantically sought to maintain its grasp upon the central government. The recovery of a few hundreds of fugitive slaves from the Seminoles is said to have finally cost as many millions as either of Napoleon's Austrian campaigns. The acquisition of Texas he calls the Nessus-shirt in which slavery was strangled. President Polk probably thought by taking George Bancroft into his cabinet to cover up his knavish practices and appear to posterity in a favorable light; but he did not count upon Von Holst, who exposes the villany of his administration as unmercifully as Tacitus that of the bad emperors. It would appear that no case of more disgusting oppression of a weak nation by a strong one than the Mexican War has been known in modern times. After that came the last futile effort at compromise, with the fugitive slave law in it like a bombshell in the family oven. Clay, Webster, and Calhoun, three Herculean statesmen, for a moment only were able to support the crazy structure, — and then went to their graves. The very next Congress overthrew their work, and the Whig party was crushed in its ruins. That such an omen portended some national catastrophe ought to have been

Introduction.

plain to the very dullest souls, for a well-established political party will commonly live for several decades after its apparent *raison d'être* has passed away.

Out of the ashes of the Whig party arose the Republican party, vigorous and resplendent in the new morning. Affairs however, had to grow worse before they could become better. The central government, in the hands of the most unscrupulous men who have ever disgraced it, lost more and more the respect of the masses in all sections of the country. The President himself became an object of derision. Courts of law were transformed into partisan engines of political corruption. The arrogance and brutality of the slavocracy culminated in the murderous assault upon an United States Senator. Hell itself seems to have been enacted in Kansas, where the central government sought to impose slavery by force upon the refractory

Northerners. What can be more distressing than that poor men should be driven from their homes with the connivance of that government which was constituted to protect them? Amid such confusion there arose a grand character, John Brown, of Ossawatomie, the central figure of this gloomy period, who took the sword of justice into his own hand, but was afterward crushed by entering into a conflict with conventional right. Von Holst has honored this unique hero (and himself at the same time), by writing a separate essay upon him, published in Vol. XLI. of the "Preussische Jahrbücher," Berlin.

Professor von Holst is no writer of panegyrics. His tone is cool, judicial, dispassionate. He rarely rises to eloquence, and whenever his subject happens to be a dry one he goes steadily through it with genuine scientific patience. Neither does he waste time on biography. The analytical tendency of his work leads him in other directions, and many a person who deserves recognition in American history receives from him merely a brief notice, or perhaps none at all. The more remarkable therefore is the special prominence which he gives to this plain, uneducated backwoodsman. The picture of John Brown he draws for us is no splendid Italian ideal, but rather a realistic German wood-cut, like those of Dürer, in which no wrinkle is smoothed over, no angularity softened. Such a portrait wins our confidence, for it appeals directly to our sense of veracity. A friend of ours once suggested that Carlyle was the one person to have written a life of John Brown, if fortunately he had happened to be acquainted with him. No doubt Carlyle would, for his was a literary genius of the highest order, and of all writers of that time he was the most like John Brown in his own nature. He could not however have explained the relation of Brown to American politics as Von Holst has done it, for politics proper Carlyle neither cared for nor understood, except in an elementary way. History was to him a grand drama, in which only the most notable events and the most distinguished actors were interesting; but to Von Holst it evidently appears as currents great and small of human life, modified by the action of prominent individuals.

It is in tracing out these currents, as an explorer determines the geographical position of an unknown river, that Von Holst's chief excellence consists. The chapter in his constitutional history on the rise of the anti-slavery movement, is a capital illustration of this. He follows it from its fountain to the broad current in which he discovers John Brown, like a great cataract forcing the waters rapidly onward to their final disappearance in the broad ocean of emancipation. This unequalled importance of the man he appreciates fully; but does he also appreciate that superior quality in Brown's nature, — the single-minded earnestness of this grim old Puritan, which won for him so readily the confidence of Emerson and Parker and Andrew, cultured men of the best American type? Von Holst does not mention this, but he says: "The man of flesh and bone led a life such as many thousands of Americans, who from the cradle almost are left to shift for themselves, still lead to-day; but the man whom God had chosen as a mortal vessel for his immortal spirit, led alongside of this life another life, of which a few only were cognizant." This is certainly a strong hint of something uncommon in the man, — either genius or exceptional character.

It is in under-estimating the importance

of his Kansas work that Von Holst, if at all, fails to do him full justice. As twenty years earlier John Quincy Adams, the true hero of his period, fought and won alone the first battle against the slavocracy by fearlessly insisting on the right of petition in Congress, — an action which Von Holst celebrates in his most spirited manner, — so was John Brown, and the Eastern friends who supported him, the first to organize armed resistance to the illegal aggression of the slavocracy in Kansas. If one marked an epoch in our history, so did the other none the less. As Atherton's gag-law was a blow aimed at the foundation of constitutional right, likewise the Atchison invasion was a bombshell fired at the pillars of constitutional government. We have the testimony of an Englishman, a relative of Mr. Gladstone, — presumably an impartial witness, — that while the pro-slavery invaders of Kansas were insolent and audacious in an extreme degree, the Free-State people seemed to lack even the confidence and resolution requisite for self-protection. No wonder it was so, when the former were encouraged by the President of the nation, and the latter found to their horror that the laws which they venerated, and which had always before protected them, were now become their enemy.

Those only who have been tossed about in an earthquake might appreciate this sensation. Then is the time for firm hearts and indomitable wills. It is a fearful moment in the consciousness of a community, — the quick transition from peaceable protest to the use of death-dealing weapons. It must not come too soon or too late. John Brown effected this transition, not only for Kansas but for the whole nation. His little battles of Black Jack and Ossa- watomie correspond in a surprising manner to Concord Bridge and Bunker Hill; as Pottawatomie, also, to the State Street massacre in Boston. The Missourians were taught that shooting was a game which both sides could play at. John Brown set an example which Lane, Montgomery, and others soon imitated with advantage. The first shot he fired was the signal of a new era in American history, and it electrified the whole country as only Adams had done once before. To obey the laws is often difficult; to break them is easy; but to rise above them is nobility itself. On the whole, however, Von Holst's account of John Brown is the best that has yet seen the light, — the most impartial and the most discriminating; and it would be unreasonable to expect everything in a single essay. No other has shown so profound an insight of the man and his historical relations.

In conclusion, it would be only just to

remark that this essay was published in Berlin before Dr. von Holst had an opportunity to examine the latest biography of John Brown. In a private letter he says of it: "In the main, my views of Brown's character and the historical significance of his career have undergone no change, though the new materials brought to light by Mr. Sanborn render some corrections as to details necessary." The details in this case are fortunately not essential. The individual acts of such a man are like the strokes of the sculptor; it is not the chips which interest us, but the whole statue. We anxiously await Von Holst's opinion of that, because he has proved himself to be, and is now everywhere admitted, a competent critic of the actions of men. In these words he gives his final judgment: "Millions of eyes were fastened on him in anxious expectation, to see whether he would not betray at the last moment that he was wearing a mask, even though this mask might be woven of the thinnest gauze wire; but after he had stood ten minutes like a statue, with the rope around his neck and the cap drawn over his eyes, the millions drew a deep breath, — he was wholly pure, wholly true. And this is why John Brown's life and death struck the minds and consciences of the North with a far mightier blow than the Lundys, Garrisons, and Douglases could deal with their most heartfelt speeches." I have lately heard an opinion similar to this last from a veteran lawyer of Boston, one of the most highly respected members of the Suffolk Bar.

As intimated already, of the various biographies of John Brown the one by Sanborn is decidedly the best. Redpath's was written at a time when full information in regard to Brown's life could scarcely be obtained, and though it served well enough the purpose of the moment, and was composed in an excellent spirit, is too much in the style of the daily pressman to be quite worthy of its subject. Another biography written by a Dr. Webb of Dublin, Ireland, appears to have been constructed upon hearsay, and is quite untrustworthy. Mr. Sanborn's "Life and Letters of John Brown," however, is a work based throughout on documentary evidence. During twenty years or more, Mr. Sanborn collected all possible information in regard to his hero in Kansas, Massachusetts, Ohio, Virginia, — wherever John Brown had lived and worked and suffered. He has placed this evidence before the reader in a plain, sincere manner, without embellishment or reservation. If its details are sometimes found to be tedious, they will always be valuable to the student of history. They give a faithful impression of the hard, toilsome, Spartan life of the man, which disciplined him so well for his last great struggle with the slave power. What we miss in it, I think, is an adequate explanation of the internal man, — the informing spirit of John Brown himself. There are glimpses of this here and there through the book, but not enough to produce a deep impression. What Mr. Sanborn substitutes for it — namely, that his hero was a special instrument of the divine will, one to whom God made his purposes directly known — is rather a *deus ex machina*, and is not likely to be credited in a critical era such as our own. It is true that Brown appears to have believed this himself; but men of action as well as poets too frequently ascribe to an external impulse what is nothing more than the sudden concentration of their own mental forces. But who will explain to us those grandly reticent natures who never explain themselves? Shakspere, who explains to us everything else in human nature, says nothing of them. Milton may have given us a hint in Samson Agonistes; and in that far off Grecian morning of man's intellectual life, there is the Prometheus of Æschylus. We see their forms upon the ceiling of the Sistine Chapel; we behold them with wonder and admiration, but we do not know them.

JOHN BROWN,

AN ESSAY BY HERMANN VON HOLST.

*Farewell God bless you
Your Friend
John Brown*

JOHN BROWN.

WHEN the spring sun has gained so much power that the snow-fields of the mountains begin to send rivulets into the valley, destruction threatens from every cliff and crag. The report of a gun, a loud call, are said to be sufficient to push over the ridge a small mass of snow, which as it falls grows to an avalanche, and may cover up whole villages.

In the same way it happens sometimes in the life of nations that things have been slowly growing ripe for a catastrophe, which is finally brought about by a deed whose significance, considered in itself, stands in ridiculous contrast to its world-wide effects.

Thus the same act which changed the United States of America from a rapidly decaying union of States into a federal union, such as would live and prosper, rendered a violent disruption of the republic inevitable in the future. But although three generations passed away before the fates could be accomplished, yet the almost insanely rash undertaking of a high-minded enthusiast proved in a single night that the time was come in which they *must* be accomplished with inconceivable horror.

The new Constitution which went into effect in 1789 founded the structure of the State on two opposing principles. The Union, in accordance with actually existing, legally sanctioned conditions and after the pattern of the separate States, was organized as a moderate democratic republic whose constituent members enjoyed complete equality before the law. But at the same time, — and here again in accordance with the actual state of things, — the Constitution recognized the existence of negro slavery in most of the States as a fact which it took into account in various ways, going even so far as to enter into positive engagements without reserving in regard to this fact adequate rights for the federal government. The development of the liberal democracy and of the diametrically opposed slavocracy proceeded simultaneously. However, in accordance with the nature of such things, the former principle spread much more rapidly, in the literal and in the metaphorical sense of the word, both because it was common to all parts of the Union, and because it was only through this principle that the powers of the individual could attain their highest development. But, on the other hand, it was just as much in the nature of things that the slave-holders should more and more get control of the Union,— partly because they were indissolubly bound together by an interest to which they subordinated everything else, and partly because by favor of this interest they maintained themselves against the federal government and against the free States on important legal rights, without binding themselves to the performance of corresponding duties. The more rapid the growth of the free North in population, wealth, culture, and morality, the more abject grew the servility of a portion of the Northern politicians toward the great Southern slave-holders; and the more boundless the despotism of the latter, the more certainly, swiftly did they see the day of their ruin approach. Each new victory placed them in a more violent and more hopeless opposition, not only to the majority of the North and to the fundamental spirit of the federal Constitution, but also to all the traditions and institutions of the slave States, in so far as they were not the outgrowth of slavery. Through the activity of the liberal democratic spirit, the Union became gradually consolidated into a national State; and slavery, which grew continually more prominent as the leading principle in the Southern States and the main interest in national politics, became every day more and more an impossibility in this national State, whether from an economical, a political, a social, or a moral point of view.

The slave-holders, who were too weak to withstand the irresistible development of existing conditions, were yet strong enough to grasp the political power, and they dragged the Union into their service with ever increasing recklessness, while at the same time they more and more unconditionally denied that the Union was competent in matters connected with slavery. They hammered hard to consolidate the federal republic, and they tore with brutal violence all binding threads into loose filaments, — and all for the service of the "peculiar institution." The more wildly they dragged the Union to the right, the more pitilessly were they obliged to goad it to the left. Slavery—which was especially fed by the constantly increasing demand for cotton — was like wildfire on a dry prairie, arousing by its own heat the whirlwind which drives it madly onward, but at the same time spending itself the more rapidly, the more irresistibly it rushes on.

The struggle of the principle of freedom with the slavocratic principle was expressed most clearly in the contest over territorial extension; and the beginning of the end was at hand when the South, in order to make good its claims, had to tear down with its own hands the barriers which it had erected thirty years before by its utmost efforts. The constant acquisition of new territory was for the South a condition of existence, for the only possible method of cultivating the land by the labor of slaves, systematically reduced to the condition of brutes, was one that exhausted the soil; and the much more rapid growth of the free North made an artificial increase of the number of slave-holding States a necessity, since the continuance of the Southern rule was bound up with the maintenance of an even balance of the parties in the federal Senate. However, the territory which the South had acquired by the purchase of Louisiana from France, in 1803, and by the Florida treaty with Spain, in 1819, had already been brought into play, while the already far more powerful North had still an immeasurable extent of land to fall back upon. The annexation of Texas, which had been contended for by the South during sixteen years with the greatest persistence and with much skill, but greatly at the expense of the country's honor, again drew the tongue of the balance more to the side of the slave-holders in 1845. But appetite grows with what it feeds on; and although Texas was as large as a good-sized kingdom, it could not long counterpoise the natural growth of the North. Mexico had threatened to consider the annexation a *casus belli*; and when, feeling its powerlessness, it failed to fulfil its threat, the United States forced on the war in order to carry the star-spangled banner and, as the South thought, slavery also, to the Pacific shore. Calhoun, who as Secretary of State had brought about the annexation of Texas, threw his whole weight as senator against this unrighteous war of conquest. He was the living personification of the slavocratic instinct, and he recognized the fact that, were the policy of the annexationists to triumph, the slave-holders would be inflicting on themselves a fearful and perhaps a fatal wound. His warning was unheeded. The blinded clan dashed past their great-minded leader, whose fears were fulfilled more completely than he himself had anticipated. While in the far West iron and lead did their bloody work, in Congress freedom and slavery wrestled for the territory which it was expected would be acquired. The Southerners succeeded, with the help of their Northern partisans, in preventing a decisive settlement of the parliamentary contest. An immense territory was added to the Union by the treaty of peace; and the attempt to secure this territory against the introduction of slavery by a resolution of Congress, was not successful. But the population of California and of New Mexico demanded, with a majority amounting almost to unanimity, to be allowed to ward this curse from their borders. The struggle for the annexed territory raged anew, and this time with a violence which shook the Union to its deepest foundations. Calhoun, worn out by grief and cares, died before a decision was reached. Daniel Webster thought he could pave his way to the White House by lowering himself to hold the stirrup of the slavocracy. He tried to clutch a shadow, and lost the respect of those who thought that such a mess of pottage as the presidency was too small a price for freedom and loyalty to principle. The gray-haired Henry Clay hastened once more from his quiet Ashland to the Senate, and devoted his dying energies to patching up the cloak which was dropping to pieces like rotten tinder, with still more rotten rags. This great undertaking succeeded. After six months' tremendous labor the so-called compromise of 1850 saw the light. It was a bargain, like all the previous bargains that were falsely called compromises; the free North was

John Brown. 65

despoiled of much that formed a part of its most sacred rights and highest interests; but still the slave-holders had not succeeded in getting all they wanted, and the chasm which irreconcilable contradictions of principle had opened between North and South, yawned broader than ever, and the web of sophistical formulas and phrases which should have bridged it over was more transparent and flimsy than ever. The mass of politicians, however, in both camps grew loudly jubilant over the eternal peace. Both parties were pledged to the compromise in the most formal fashion by the politicians who met in the national conventions.

If only words could have done away with disagreeable facts! The extreme wings of both parties grew very bitter over the conditions of this penny-wise transaction, conditions which were alike dishonorable and impossible of fulfilment; and the contradiction between the promises of the compromise and the actual state of affairs grew constantly greater. The sweat was scarcely dry on the brows of the worn-out politicians when they were forced to work with busy hands to loosen the knots of the highly artistic net which they had woven with so much pains. The compromise had been a heavy blow for the North, but the South had not won by its means any new territory for slavery. California had been admitted as a free State (Statutes at Large, ix., 452), and the question as to the right to hold slaves in New Mexico and Utah had been silently passed over as long as they remained Territories (Ibid. pp. 447, 453).

Whatever concessions might be made to the slave-holders, their defeat and final ruin were unavoidable if they remained confined within their then boundaries. But what had just happened in California opened to them a melancholy prospect in case the question were left open until the Territories were received as States into the Union; for there the members of the convention to draft a Constitution, even those of Southern origin, had voted unanimously to exclude slavery. The slave-holders' party must make sure of the Territories if it wished later to have control over the States. The radical leaders of the party therefore maintained that slavery and freedom were equally lawful in all the Territories of the Union, and that no political power had the right to exclude slavery. But even their most devoted adherents in the North would not agree to this, and even the more moderate Southern politicians refused to deny in so brazen a fashion a principle which the great Southern statesmen had always recognized as law and had used as a guide for their actions. But the men who wished for peace at any price and the politicians who thought that the Southern party was most likely to favor their reckless ambition were absolutely sure of one thing ; namely, that the raging South must be satisfied. They sought to escape from the dilemma by means of the doctrine whose promulgation is erroneously ascribed to Senator Stephen Douglas, of Illinois, — the doctrine of the so-called squatter sovereignty. According to this doctrine Congress could neither forbid slavery in the Territories nor introduce it there; on the other hand, the squatters should have the right to decide whether they would allow slavery or not. This is not the place to set forth the utter nonsense of this doctrine, whether from a constitutional or from a political point of view. The majority of Congress adopted it and thereby overthrew the Missouri compromise. This compact, which forever prohibited slavery north of 36° 31', had hitherto been recognized by all parties without distinction as peculiarly sacred and as binding for all time. In its stead the law of nature was now set, — the *bellum omnium contra omnes.* Kansas Territory was the first battle-field. No law existed there in regard to slavery. Events alone were to decide. That side was to win which within a certain time could bring the greatest number of followers into the Territory. Under these conditions the North took up the fight, and its great superiority was soon demonstrated. But the South contrived to find crutches on which to support its weakened limbs. On election days hundreds of "roughs," armed to the teeth, poured into the Territory from the Missouri border, cast as many ballots as they pleased into the ballot boxes, from which they scared away the real squatters by threats or open violence, and won in this way an easy and brilliant victory. As the federal executive had pledged itself body and soul to the slave-holders, the only recourse of the champions of freedom was to oppose violence with violence. Neither right nor policy could decide the question whether the Territory should belong to the democratic republic of free labor or should be handed over to barbarism under the Moloch of slavery. The freebooters of the "party of law and order," led by a former Vice-President of the Union, proved by means of bowie-knives, revolvers, shotguns, and even cannon that "slavery is the broadest and surest foundation for a free existence;" and the Free-Soil men proved with the same arguments that the people of the North had not yet completely lost their common-sense and their manliness in the voluptuous embrace of the strumpet slavery, and under the poisonous breath of her burning kisses. The "irrepressible conflict" between slavery and freedom was

John Brown. 71

carried from the forum of absolute right to the judgment seat of the God of battles; but the God of battles in the civilized world of Christianity is the God of righteousness also, the God of truth, the God of moral principles, and the God of freedom. For eighty years the opposing spirits had fought, and now the personal encounter was to begin. North and South tried their strength on the soil of Kansas; and a civil war arose as fruitful of baseness and horror as any civil war of other times. But the people of the North found their better selves again in the blood which drenched the soil of Kansas. They awoke once more to the consciousness that laws exist for man, and not man for the laws, and that the nation was bound neither in the eyes of man nor in the eyes of God to allow itself to be politically and morally ruined for the sake of the laws. As citizens, as members of the political community, they could no longer come to an understanding as to law and right; and as men — as men in whose hearts and brains there was yet a spark of the divine spirit — they bade the citizen draw back. Yea, they rose up in rebellion against him, and cut with the sword the knot which law and right could no longer unravel.

It was in December, 1855. A large armed force, consisting mostly of Missourians, but nevertheless passing for Kansas militia and marching under the authority of the federal government, appeared before Lawrence, the principal town of the Free-Soil men of the territory. The townspeople prepared to resist, and their partisans from the surrounding country hastened to bring them aid. A small troop of these auxiliaries attracted especial attention. They drove up in front of the Free States Hotel in a lumber-wagon. Rods were fixed in the sides of the wagon, and from these rods bayonets projected into the air. The men stood upright with improved rifles in their hands, and their belts bristling with well-selected weapons. Four were young, one or two were scarcely more than boys; in their midst stood a man fifty-five years old. John Brown and four sons — two others had to remain behind for the time on account of sickness — came at the call of the Lord of hosts to fight out a life-and-death struggle with slavery, — " the sum of all iniquities." He was almost six feet high, and slender rather than stout. His body, though not broad in the shoulders, told of unusual strength. The muscles and sinews seemed to be woven with threads of iron. The hair, which had grown gray with years, stood up in a dense mass above the high forehead, which retreated somewhat in its upper part. Two deep furrows, telling of thought and cares, ran down between the bushy eyebrows to the strong, curved nose. The thick, full beard could not conceal the firm closing of the lips of the broad mouth. The large clear eyes seemed to change color from the intensity of the fire that glowed in them,—sometimes they appeared light blue; sometimes dark gray, sometimes black. When he hastened on with a rapid and remarkably energetic gait, making room for no one that he met, his head would be slightly bent forward and his eye cast down, as though he were lost in serious thought. But his eyes seemed to pierce to the uttermost depths when he fixed them on a face; and if the enemy was near, they turned restlessly hither and thither, as though no point of the horizon should escape them for even a single moment.

The man had led a busy and agitated life; but he had never come into public notice. Finding pleasure in his calling, he devoted himself to it quietly but with great activity. He was no dreamer, and not even an enthusiast in the ordinary sense of the word. An American through and through, Nature had formed him for vigorous work, and the vicissitudes of his life had developed his natural inclination to a high degree. The man of flesh and bone led a life such as thousands and thousands of Americans, left to shift for themselves almost from the cradle, still lead to-day; but the man whom God had chosen as a mortal vessel for his immortal spirit, led alongside of this life another, of which very few outside of his family circle knew anything, and they had only a faint idea of it. The sandy sea-shore presents year after year the same appearance, though mighty waves may rush foaming over it ever so often; but the paths which the trickling stream makes for itself in the hidden recesses of the cliffs remain, even though no human eye sees them, and the parched wanderer in the burning sunlight asks perhaps chidingly why Nature gives the barren rock no water. The Brown whom neighbors and friends had known for half a century, had bravely tossed about on the stormy sea of American business life, but the waters had gone as they had come. That which was to make of him a figure in the world's history lay unnoticed and mostly unknown in the quiet depths of his soul. The deed of his life sprang from a spirit as guileless, as pure, as true, and as unselfish as that of a child; but it was performed by a man whose every fibre had been steeled by the stern discipline of life, and whose inner being was so absolutely ruled by the categorical imperative that his will could neither be broken nor bent. Tender and soft as a girl who nestles in her mother's lap, and yet every inch a man; as ignorant of the power of actual facts as a hermit in the desert, and at the same time wonderfully fitted by nature and training to seize the best chance at first sight under the most difficult circumstances, and to accomplish the most with the smallest means; illogical as a child, and yet following his own path as steadily as the sun; with a horror of fighting, and yet offering up himself and his family in an insane war against the whole nation; so tenderhearted that he stakes and loses his own life and the life of his followers, of his sons-in-law and sons, merely to save a few strangers from their anxiety lest the train with their relatives should not arrive at the right time, and at the same time so terribly stern that he unconditionally approves a horrible five-fold murder; never excited to revenge even by the worst injustice exercised toward himself and toward those dearest to him, but goaded on to such a rage by the wrong done to the negro slaves that he recklessly trangresses all positive law and only recognizes as binding what he considers to be God's command,—such is the portrait of the first man who died by the hand of the executioner for a political crime in the United States.

John Brown was born in Torrington, Litchfield County, Conn., on the 9th of May, 1800.[1] His pedigree can be traced without a single break back to Peter Brown, a joiner, and one of the "Pilgrim Fathers" whom the Mayflower landed at Plymouth Rock on the 22d of December, 1620. His grandfather John died a captain in the army of the Revolution Sept. 3, 1776, and his maternal grandfather also served in the same army. Owen Brown, the father of the martyr, moved in

[1] Not as Kapp thinks (John Brown aus und über Amerika, ii. p. 121), in northeastern New York. See Brown's Autobiography, printed in Redpath's The Public Life of Capt. John Brown, p. 24.

1805 to Hudson, Ohio, at that time one of the most remote Western settlements.

The boy soon lost his fear of the sneaking redskins. When but six years old he wandered fearlessly through the wilderness barefoot and bareheaded, with his "leather trousers held," as he writes, "sometimes by two suspenders and sometimes by one." The fare was scanty, and instruction scantier still, but in the midst of hard work and the rough games of his few comrades, his body was steeled and his wit grew keen in the school of "help yourself." His reading was as yet none of the best, and he wrote but a sorry hand; yet the twelve-year-old boy at the time of the second war with England drove alone large herds of cattle through the wilderness to camp, a hundred miles and more away. During one of these expeditions, he was extremely well received at a slaveholder's, who made much of the bold knowing boy before his guests. He remained, however, insensible to the praise bestowed upon him, because of his indignation at the harsh way in which the host treated his negro boy. He explained afterward that this occurrence had made an Abolitionist of him and had made him "swear eternal war on slavery."

It was not merely his own innate feelings that produced in him a profound aversion to slavery. However faulty his education had been as a whole, it was thorough in one respect,— he knew the Bible better than many a minister of the gospel, and he had learned to read it with all the grim puritanic earnestness which for more than two centuries had filled his race. Although he had never forgotten it, yet three and forty years went by before he entered upon the literal fulfilment of the oath which he had sworn as a boy. He always bore witness fearlessly when occasion offered; but it was for the Lord to designate the hour at which thought should be transformed into action. If there ever was a sect of Christianity who adopted equally the gospel of love of the New Testament and the stern severity of the Old Testament spirit in all its terrible grandeur, the Puritans were that sect; and if ever a Puritan exemplified the welding together of these opposite principles in his whole life, and in each and every act, John Brown was that Puritan. He was the man of the old covenant, who waited quietly and patiently to gird about his loins " the sword of Gideon" till a sign from God gave the order. And how in the nineteenth century and in one of the foremost of civilized States could that sword be a weapon suitable for the hand of a boy, or even for the grip of a man, who had not yet drunk deep of the bitter dregs of the cup of life? A youth could, indeed, have called the slaves to rebellion, but the world in the most favorable case would have looked upon him as an object of pity, who ought already to have been placed in an insane asylum. What alone caused Brown's deed to produce such a powerful and ever increasing effect North and South, was the fact that he held as a sacred tenet from first to last, without a second's doubting, the belief that he was God's chosen bearer of the sword of Gideon; but in order that such a belief should be awe-inspiring and not ridiculous, but should be fearful, it must be held by a man on whose head lay the snow of age, in whose veins the blood coursed slowly and evenly, and who could point to a long life as to an irrefutable proof that he was as cool as ice and as completely the master of his five senses as any man.

Already, as a ten-year-old boy, Brown let it be seen clearly that it was not in his power to enjoy the bright sides of life. The few books which he could get hold of, and from which he mostly got his education, were of a serious sort, and he began to prefer the society of older men to that of his comrades. Light talk, even when it was entirely inoffensive, was distasteful to him. He touched neither tobacco, cards, nor alcoholic drinks as long as he lived; yet he was not a "crank," and did not pass for such. On the contrary, he was so highly esteemed that it became a second nature with him to speak with a tone of absolute authority. He always carried through to the end whatever he undertook. He gave up his purpose of becoming a minister of the gospel only because his eyes would not stand the strain of continued study. He went back to business, tried various things in different States, and what he accomplished was always satisfactory and often excellent. He became a good tanner under his father's guidance; his sheep-raising was a model for the whole neighborhood; in the wool-trade he introduced the important graduation of wool, and as a cattle-raiser, he sent, in 1850, to an agricultural show a variety of the celebrated Devonshire "Short-horns," whose beauty caused a great sensation among the whole farming population. The business enterprises at the head of which he stood were often important and prosperous. But Fate, which had destined him for something greater, seemed to watch with anxious jealousy lest the elasticity of his muscles and the proud energy of his will should relax in the midst of ease and comfort. He lost again and again his painfully acquired property, partly through unfortunate accidents, and partly through the machinations of business friends who cared more for profit than for what was just and fair, and for whom the stern righteousness of the Puritan was an obstacle. He lost, however, what was dearer than money or estate. His first wife died in August, 1832, and in September, 1843, he buried three sons on the same day. Of the nineteen children whom his two wives bore him eight alone survived their father.

After the failure of his wool business in Springfield, Mass., Brown moved, in 1845, to North Elba in Essex County, New York. The years he spent there as a farmer were the night-watch preparatory to the deed which was to shape the course of the world's history. Gerrit Smith, one of the most distinguished Abolitionists and most high-minded philanthropists, had set apart a portion of his extensive possessions in this part of the State of New York to found a colony for free colored people. Brown offered to live among the negroes as their fatherly friend and adviser, and Smith joyfully accepted the offer. The undertaking did not succeed for various reasons, but more especially owing to the rascalities of a surveyor. Here, however, in the midst of the severe stillness of the Adirondacks, which assume at this point the character of a mighty range of rocky mountains, the spirit of Brown gazed more and more into its own depths. During the long winter evenings there was plenty of time for reading the Bible and for earnest conversation and thought in the simple shabby-looking farmhouse. His numerous family and his warm friends, the Thompsons, listened devoutly to the words of the experienced, storm-tried man, full of childlike simplicity. And when at last the sign came for which he had watched so long, he had poured out his own spirit in such wealth among this band, which crowded around him in really patriarchal simplicity and devotion, that the men followed him without his commanding or requesting them to do so, as though it were a matter of course, and the women did not seek to hold them back by a single look of entreaty.

The treason against Kansas, committed by the weak-kneed, the self-seeking, and the corrupt politicians, although the State had been pledged to freedom for all time by the fathers, was the sign long waited for by Brown that it was time for him to stand up and take his rifle. As early as 1854 his four eldest sons decided to move to Kansas. The way in which they went to work to carry out their resolution leaves no doubt that they intended to settle permanently in the Territory; but Kapp is mistaken when he says (p. 122), that the father too moved to Kansas as a peaceful farmer.[1] Accompanied by two, or as

[1] On the 18th of February, 1857, Brown told the Massachusetts Legislature that he had been summoned with six sons and a son-in-law to defend Lawrence, in May, 1856.

some have it, three other sons, he followed the call of his children, who had suffered from the Missouri border ruffians, and begged their father to hasten to their aid with arms. In the first informal examination to which Brown was subjected in prison, by Governor Wise and Senator Mason, of Virginia, and Vallandigham of Ohio, he said: "Four of my sons had gone there [to Kansas] as squatters, and they were the occasion of my going there. I did not go to settle, but on account of the difficulties."[1]

Brown went to Kansas in order to drive the partisans of slavery from the soil to which they had no right, by means of powder and shot. He was accordingly very much displeased at having come to Lawrence with his four sons for nothing, because the leading men of the place pre-

[1] The Life, Trial, and Execution of Capt. John Brown, p. 45.

ferred a slothful peace to a bold struggle. The latter, on the other hand, looked with anxious distrust on the grim old man, in whose vocabulary the word "compromise" had no place, and who knew of only one argument that would carry the day, and that was bloodshed.

The old man was right; the wise politicians were over-wise. There was no possibility of keeping on a good footing with the law, because the executors of the law knew no other compelling power than that which forced them to obey the slave-holders. It was subjection or war; there was no mean between the two extremes. And Brown saw that if the decision was war, it could not be the sort of war in which Grotius and Vattel would be always conscientiously consulted. If the enemy acted in accordance with the maxim that he who shot first and best was in the right, he too claimed the right to act according to the same principle where it was necessary. A God-fearing man, he yet did not shrink from executing the code of Judge Lynch in all its horror. After the Kansas days were past, some one asked him once, speaking of one of the worst partisans of slavery, "Well, Captain, Judge Lecompte would have had a hard time of it, I guess, if the Lord had delivered him into your hands?" The judge would doubtless have felt his blood curdle if he had heard the quiet, laconic answer, "It would have taken the Lord himself to tear him out of them again." It is at bottom only owing to a fortunate accident that his memory is not stained with a sort of court-martial execution. Five members of the slave-holders' party, who had committed great brutalities against Free-Soil people, and had warned them that if they should not have left the Territory within a given time they would be hanged, were pulled out of their beds

John Brown. 91

and put to death not far from Pottawatomie, in the night of May 24, 1856. Several witnesses declared that Brown was the leader of this band of combined prosecutors, judges, and executors.[1] It was natural to think that he was the originator of the bloody deed, as he and his sons were among those who had been threatened with the hangman's rope, and as it was his daughter and daughter-in-law who had received from the tongues and hands of the roughs, fighting for "law and order," specimens of the renowned "chivalry" of the South. The accusation was therefore perhaps brought in good faith, but it was false. Redpath heard from two of those who took part in the murder that Brown on that night was twenty-five miles away with one of his sons. Brown acknowledged this at a later period to his future biographer, but added, " Take heed, how-

[1] Congressional Globe, XXXVI. Cong., 1 Sess., p. 105.

ever, that I do not say this in order to throw guilt off from myself; although my hand was not engaged, I would have advised the step if I had known the circumstances, and I approved of it."[1]

It was, above all, this cool, reckless energy, which shrank from no consequences of the first step, that made of Brown the most dreaded leader of the men on the side of the Free-State party. Besides, he had a really remarkable talent for guerilla warfare. It may have been absurd of him to criticise minutely Napoleon's dispositions for a battle; but no one understood better than he how to post a handful of men in a wood or in a gorge so that they could keep in check a force ten times their superior, composed of such heroes as the Missouri rangers. On the 30th of August, 1856, he posted himself with about thirty men in the way of a troop of from

[1] Redpath, p. 119.

four hundred to five hundred well armed Missourians who had even brought cannon with them, and did not let them pass until he had killed more than thirty and wounded about fifty. Soon after, before Lawrence with between forty and fifty men armed with rifles, he prepared such a warm night reception for four hundred cavalry that not only the latter retreated, but also the force of about two thousand men who had burned down Franklin and were marching on Lawrence thought good to face about. However, he understood not only how to make excellent use of the lay of the land, but how to teach his people not to waste their shot. He adopted both sides of Cromwell's maxim, " Put your trust in God, and keep your powder dry." He was fully aware of the worth of his own moral superiority and of that of his people. He declared that it was foolishness to think that the square-built bullies who were the matadores at tavern brawls and on the street, and who had primed themselves with brandy, were the best material for soldiers. He said that he who defended a great and noble cause, who fought for his wife and children, and who trusted in God, could stand against ten rapscallions in the pay of hell. He put his trust in God, and each beat of his pulse spoke of the sacredness of the cause to which he had devoted his life. The day was begun and ended with prayer in his camp, and no morsel was touched before thanks had been rendered to the Giver of all good gifts. Woe to the man who uttered a profane word in his presence! Once some border roughs whom he had taken prisoners were cursing. As they were beginning to curse again in spite of his protest, he pointed his cocked revolver at them and thundered, "Kneel down and pray!" They knelt down and prayed. They had to pray more during the five days they passed in his camp than they had presumably prayed in their whole lives.

No one has ventured to assert that this stern piety was with him an acquired habit or even a blind. On his return East, late in the autumn of 1856, his opinions and belief in his God-given mission were subjected to tests which few would have endured. On Feb. 18, 1857, before a committee of the Massachusetts Legislature he said: " About the first of September (1856), myself and five sick and wounded sons and a son-in-law had to lie on the ground a long time without covering and at times almost starved, and completely thrown on the charity of the above-mentioned Christian Indian and his wife." And that was one of the lesser trials which he had to stand. " Near Black Jack," so ran his tale, "the Missourians wounded three Free-State men, — one of them was my son-in-law; a few days later one of my sons was wounded so that he will remain a cripple for life." After giving a long list of the sufferings of others which he had witnessed, he went on: " Abandoned houses and corn-fields were to be seen in almost every direction south of the Kansas River.

" However, I have not yet told all that I saw in Kansas. Once I saw three mutilated bodies; two were dead and one still lived, but was riddled with twenty bullet holes and buck-shot holes; the two murdered men had been lying eighteen hours on the ground, a prey to the flies. One of these young men was my own son."

A clergyman, Martin White by name, boasted of having shot down Frederick Brown, who, thinking to meet friends, was going on his way peaceably and unarmed.

This part of his story was hard for the old man, he could scarcely utter the words. After a few moments, however, he was again calm. He had not yet told the worst that he had to say. This was the chapter concerning his son John, which he had not committed to paper. It was short enough to be told in a few impromptu sentences. " Captain " Tate, formerly a journalist, now really a wandering knight in the service of slavery and pretending to be in the service of United-States Marshal Donaldson for the purpose of maintaining " law and order," — Captain Tate arrested John Brown, Jr., and his brother Jason, while they were peaceably attending to their business. He had no legal order to arrest them; but it seemed good to him to declare them guilty of murder and high treason on his own responsibility. They were put into chains, dragged away, and soon handed over to the United-States dragoons under Captain Wood, who made common cause with the border roughs. The dragoons with their horses drove the prisoners, laden with chains and hatless, many miles under the burning sun. John could not endure the torture: his mind got out of joint.[1] The father now asked the gentlemen of the Committee of the Legislature if they wished to see the chains; they were always with him as a memorial, he said, and were now in his hotel. As he was concluding his report of this episode with the statement that the treatment his son had suffered had made of him "a madman, — yes, a madman," his bronzed features trembled and a tear stole over his cheek.

The man who, after going through such trials, still persevered in the work which he had once for all set himself to do, and staked all that he had not yet lost, — such

[1] Phillips' The Conquest of Kansas, pp. 332, 333.

a man must either have been driven by a thirst for revenge, or he must have honestly taken himself for an instrument in God's hand which had to do its work without looking to the right or to the left. Kapp says, speaking of Brown's career in Kansas, " He takes up the fight for the right, and revenges himself as well as he can: eye for eye, tooth for tooth." It seems to me that the expression " revenges himself " is an unhappy one. True, his motto was, " Eye for eye, tooth for tooth," but merely in order to exercise justice and to protect the right. Again and again he was asked in prison whether he had wished to revenge himself for the wrong suffered by his sons, and after a moment of deep thought he always answered quietly, but with the utmost positiveness, that so far as he knew his own inner thoughts, this feeling had never filled his breast. But Brown was no actor, he did not play a part. The idea of revenge is incompatible with his whole being. The death of his sons caused him acute suffering, but it did not make him bitter, and it did not turn him from his path. We shudder when we read in the Bible how Abraham draws his knife against his son at God's bidding, and it is hard to believe that a cultivated man of the nineteenth century could give up one after the other of his sturdy sons — with tears, it is true, but without a murmur and without the slightest hesitation — because his "mission" required it. And yet John Brown really thought and felt in this way.

Whenever I have stood among the ruins of the classic age, before a single column which had once been one of many to support the roof of a temple, I have always had a feeling as though I stood before a sort of enigma. This picture involuntarily came to me while trying to grasp the mental and moral nature of this remarkable man. In his comparisons he was fond of referring to the Bible accounts of Old Testament heroes. He bore the imprint of their spirit. All who did not believe what they believed, were devoted to the sword. In Brown's eyes, the man who saw slavery under any other aspect than that of a moral wrong, was a heathen. His platform is a narrow one, a very narrow one; but on this platform he stands, towering up mightily in genuine grandeur, — a solitary pillar in this sober world, with its calmly analytic thought, and its broad and shallow thread-bare sentiment. But how did this representative of a long-vanished period of civilization come into this modern world of ours? There is only one explanation. Negro slavery, as it had developed in the United States, on the soil of the most democratic State in the world, which in all other respects was even with the times, was itself so much of an anachronism and an anomaly that the whole history of the world cannot produce its fellow.

So far Brown had stood on the defensive; he had only helped to defend Kansas from being overpowered by the party of the slave-holders. His return to the East was the decisive turning-point in his life. He had not come to seek rest and relaxation. He had taken the final resolve to assume the offensive, and he wished to collect in the East the necessary material aid. He travelled about, knocked at many doors where he thought that he could count not merely upon sympathetic words, but also upon effective assistance; here and there he spoke in public meetings; he even published in the papers a call for assistance. But the contributions came in very scantily. In a written "Farewell to the Plymouth Rocks, Bunker Hill Monuments, Charter Oaks, and Uncle Tom's Cabins," he summons "the glorious Commonwealth" before the judgment seat of God, on account of its lukewarmness in a cause "in which every man, woman, and child, yea, in which the whole human race has a deep and awful interest." He was again on his way to Kansas as early as June, 1857, but he did not get there till November, because lack of money forced him to interrupt his journey.

However, his stay in the East had by no means been barren of results. He had formed new connections, he had drawn old ties closer, and the object of it all was to collect a small band of men who were ready to burn their ships and to begin with him the holy war of extermination against slavery. He had already selected Harper's Ferry as the point where the first great blow was to be struck. A certain Forbes, however, who was to have been a drill-sergeant for his people, and who later on betrayed him, persuaded him for the time to give up this idea. For the present, Kansas was to continue to be the scene of his exploits. It is not necessary to go into the details of what he did there. His life was agitated enough, but he did not experience as many remarkable vicissitudes as the first year. The main thing was the silent inward and outward preparation for his coming grand raid on Virginia. One event alone deserves special mention.

Brown carried "the war into Africa" for the first time in December, 1858. Dividing his force into two parts, he went with his associates over the borders of Missouri, freed eleven slaves, and took them to Kansas. The division led by his friend Kagi shot down a man who levelled his gun at the invaders, and

Brown took as much money from the slave-holders as, according to his estimate, would suffice to pay for the work which the slaves had hitherto done. This characterizes completely the procedure which he intended henceforth to observe. He does not at all consider himself called upon to punish the slave-holders. He merely wants to assist the slave in getting what is his due. But he shoots down any one who forcibly resists him. He only added one other point to this programme, — at first he lightened the purse of his victims only to make up the wages which were owing to the slaves; later on he thought it just and fair that they should furnish him the means to free other slaves.

This raid made a great sensation. The Governor of Missouri offered a reward of $3000, and the President a further reward of $250, for the capture of Brown. But he brought his charges in good condition to Canada, after putting to flight with only eight men, and without firing a shot, more than forty Missourians who pursued him. It was a natural and completely justifiable view of the situation that both sides considered this event as much more important than the biggest "battle" which had been fought in Kansas. The appearance of a highwayman armed to the teeth — if I may allow myself a comparison from the Southern point of view — throws the whole region into frightful excitement, while the sneak thieves, though they may cause much more damage, are quietly left to the local police, so long as things are not carried quite too far. What do the eleven slaves freed by Brown signify when compared with the great number of those whom the Abolitionists and freed slaves had already been conveying every year for a long time by the so-called "underground railroad," to the British possessions? It was the fact that an armed band had entered a slave State and forcibly freed a number of slaves; and this startled the whole South like a bursting bombshell. It is true that Southerners had often allowed themselves to resort to the most violent methods of propagating their "peculiar institution;" but they would sooner have believed that the heavens were falling than that the Northern "doughfaces" and "mudsills" could return the compliment. And they showed at once how very conscious they were of the fact that the "peculiar institution" which they called the corner-stone of their greatness, was in reality sadly weakening in its effects. The border counties of Missouri lost for some time their craving for expeditions against Kansas, and those who owned slaves hastened to sell them farther from the border. In one district, which at the time of Brown's first raid had had five hundred slaves, there were only fifty to be found two years later. It was certainly easier to protect one's self in this way against the old man than to earn the rewards that had been offered for him. And the slave-holders were right in taking for granted that he would not be satisfied with this one success. He now started an organization in Canada for the purpose of reducing to a system the work of freeing the slaves, and of accomplishing it on a large scale.

A convention of Abolitionists radical enough to inspire Brown with confidence, was called together with great secrecy, and met in Chatham, West Canada, on the 8th of April, 1859. The place of meeting was a negro church, and a colored clergyman, named Munroe, presided. Brown laid before the convention a paper drawn up by himself and entitled, "Provisional Constitution and Ordinances for the people of the United States." This document was a confused medley of absurd, because absolutely inapplicable, forms, and of measures well calculated for the end in view,— of sound common-sense and of absurd systematizing; of cool computation and of inconceivable over-estimates of the resources at hand; of true, keen-sighted humanity and of reckless severity. It was absurd in itself that a little band of negroes and a few white men without influence should secretly put their heads together in Canada in order to give a Constitution to the people of the United States; but it was entirely rational to create a strong organization which had for its object the breaking of the chains of the slaves. It was absurd for this corporal's guard of officers with no troops behind them to copy the Federal Constitution and to desire a President with a complete cabinet, a Congress "with not less than five, nor more than ten members," a Supreme Court and four lower courts; but it was entirely sensible to appoint a supreme commander; that is, to place all the means available in the hands of one man. It was hard that all those who willingly kept slaves, all enemies, and all who assisted the enemy, should have all they possessed taken away from them, "wherever found, whether in free or in slave-holding States." But in the case of these fanatics the fact deserves to be acknowledged, that they would recognize any kind of neutrality, that they promised not to execute any prisoner without a fair trial, and a verdict of the court strictly forbade all useless destruction of property, and would not unnecessarily wound the feelings of the defeated enemy even with a single word. This plan was probably intended for moral effect on the emancipated negroes, to hold them under some restraint during confusion. It was a piece of insanity, in the literal sense of the word, to create such a government and to want to carry on such a war, and yet to declare that there was no intention of overthrowing the state or federal government; but it showed that in a few instances the conspirators saw farther than their noses, that they would not be content with the freeing of the slaves, but promised also to look out for the bringing together again of separated families, for schools and even for the furtherance of "personal cleanliness." The plan was so nonsensical that it was an unseemly piece of pleasantry on the part of the Attorney-General to accuse Brown later of high treason, and on the part of the jury to declare him guilty, because he had set up a government of his own by means of this "Provisional Constitution." But the fact that a society had been formed which practically intrusted all its means to a supreme commander (whatever powers were given on paper to the Secretary of the Treasury and to Congress), and that John Brown was unanimously chosen supreme commander, — this fact was important enough.

An ill-boding sultriness filled the air of the whole Commonwealth. The decision of the Supreme Court in the Dred Scott Case, which opened to slavery the whole territorial domain of the Union, was a dearly bought victory for the South. The just exasperation of the Republicans spurred them on to increased efforts, while the split in the Democratic party made ceaseless and rapid progress. President Buchanan presented daily a more pitiful spectacle of moral wretchedness; daily it seemed more probable that the Republicans would carry the next presidential election; and constantly did the Southern Hotspurs declare that the day on which a Republican was chosen President would be the last day of the Union.

Who, at this stage of affairs, would have thought of the bold leader of volunteers during the times of "bleeding Kansas"? In the United States more than anywhere else, people live in the present, and Brown was not at all anxious to remind the public of his existence. Diligently, but with the greatest secrecy, he made his preparations.

In the State of Virginia, on the left bank of the Potomac, lies the town of Harper's Ferry, which Brown had had in mind years before. Brown wanted to explode his first big mine in Virginia, because this State had always held in the South the leading position, although the centre of the slave-holders' power lay in the cotton States, where the radical wing of the party was consequently strongest. And Brown had chosen Harper's Ferry as the centre of operations, partly because there was an important United-States Arsenal in the place, and partly because it lay near the mountains, which offered hiding-places enough, and many points which a band of resolute men could easily defend against a superior force. The choice of just this place was therefore by no means so unfortunate and so unwise as has often been asserted.

Toward the end of June there appeared at Harper's Ferry a " Mr. Smith " and his two sons, who came, as they said, to look for a farm, being tired of farming in western New York, where the frosts had repeatedly destroyed the crops. The stranger, who presented a striking appearance by reason of his long beard, hired the Kennedy farm after looking about a little. When he had taken possession, a few other men joined him, one by one. The neighbors wondered a little that the new-comers did not seem to have any regular occupation, and that, though they often went into the mountains to hunt, they never brought home any game. They remarked also that large chests were repeatedly brought into the quiet house. But as the occupants paid for everything in cash, and showed themselves friendly, helpful neighbors, they were not troubled by curious intruders, and no heed was given to the strangers who often dropped in upon them.

On the night of October 16, the picture changed as though by magic. The game which Smith was out after, fell into his hands without having cost him a grain of powder. No shot had been fired, no cry had broken the stillness of the night, and yet Brown was in possession of the arsenal, guards occupied the railroad bridge which leads to the Maryland shore of the river, the faithful Kagi was bringing in as a prisoner Colonel Washington, whom he had captured with his arms and negroes, the watchmen were safely locked up in the watch house, the telegraph wires were cut, and the rails torn up. Even the first shot at midnight failed to alarm the slumbering town. It was fired at a watchman who had come to relieve the watch at the railroad bridge, and who, on being summoned to surrender, ran off. It was only when the train which arrived a little after one o'clock could not get through, that the sleepers were roughly made aware that something extraordinary was going on. The railroad officials of the train, who wanted to cross the bridge on foot, turned round at sight of the levelled rifles. A man trying to follow the example of the watchman, who had luckily escaped, was shot down. It was a bad omen that in this foolhardy war, undertaken for the slaves, the first man who fell at the hands of the insurgents was a negro. But this was not all. Brown's moderate command had been transgressed. He had ended his last speech to his people with the words: " Do not take a human life if you can by any means avoid it, but if you must take another's life to save your own, then aim well." He repelled afterward the accusation of murder with the assertion that he only made use of his weapons in self-defence. The killing of this negro was brought up against him, and he had to be responsible for all that his associates had done, even against his orders.

But whatever may be attributed to the mistakes of his associates, it was undoubtedly Brown who brought down destruction upon himself. He sealed his fate by accompanying the train over the bridge toward morning, allowing it to proceed on its way, and yet going back quietly into the buildings he had seized. Steam and electricity carried in a few hours the astounding news to the uttermost borders of the country. Armed bodies of men marched against him from all sides,— not merely the militia of Virginia and Maryland, but also regular troops of the Federal army,— and he remained motionless at his post with his sixteen white men and five negroes. Did he believe that the hosts of heaven would descend to cleave for him, with their flaming swords, a broad path through the ranks of the swarming enemy, who had it in their power to surround Harper's Ferry so closely that not a mouse could escape? This he did not believe, however positively he assumed that the arm of the Lord was above him. Was he obliged to remain? No; he was still completely master of the situation. Though his company had only twenty-two rifles all told, the inhabitants of the place were so paralyzed by fear that he could have reached the shelter of the mountains with certainty, and possibly without loss. Was he not aware that, like a fox, he would soon be surrounded in his camp by a countless pack of hounds? Certainly he was aware of it, for when he took the eleven slaves out of Missouri, he said that the inhabitants of the State had "hounded all hell against him," and he could hardly imagine that his enemies would remain idle lookers-on. Why then did he stay? Was it an obstinate clinging to the plan which he had once for all marked out for himself? Again the answer is no. His plan by no means required that he should maintain his position at Harper's Ferry. Then what in the world chained his footsteps? It is impossible to give a clear and certain answer to this question, for not even Brown was ever able to answer it to himself in a satisfactory manner. It is as though during these decisive hours a thick veil had fallen over the eyes that were wont to see so clearly. On the 15th of November he writes from prison to his old teacher, the Rev. H. L. Vaill: "I have felt very much disappointed in myself because I did not hold fast to my own plans; but now I am entirely reconciled, for God's plan was beyond a doubt much better, otherwise I should have held to my own. If Samson had remained true to his resolve not to tell Delilah wherein his great strength lay, he probably never would have pulled down the house. I told Delilah nothing, but I was driven to act very much against my better judgment."

The first manifestations of uncertainty on the part of Brown seem to have been due to the fact that he felt himself obliged to strike his blow earlier than he at first intended. Redpath declares that the 24th of October had been definitely appointed for the attack. On that day, as he says, a number of friends from the United States and from Canada were to have joined Brown, but the news that Forbes had warned the President drove him to immediate action. There is presumably some truth in the story; but Redpath's heated imagination sees the whole raid through a powerful magnifying-glass, and he wants to avenge the friend whom he honored like a saint, by trying to make the South believe that Brown had really laid a huge network of mines which, in spite of his execution, would soon explode into the air.

The main reason why Brown, as soon as he had brought the arsenal into his power, remained doubtingly expectant, entirely contrary to his nature, lay much deeper.

Mason of Virginia declared later that at least fifteen or twenty thousand dollars' worth of arms had been found in Brown's house, and that he carried with him "a large sum of money in gold."[1] This is a wanton exaggeration. There were found, besides a few things not worth mentioning, one hundred and two rifles and twelve pistols, with a considerable amount of ammunition, four hundred and eighty-three pikes, fifty-five old bayonets, and twelve artillery sabres; and as to the large sum of money, it would at the outside have sufficed to support a battalion for a day.[2] These preparations scarcely indicated that the Union was in danger of being lifted from its foundations. Still Brown undoubtedly counted on a considerable addition to his force, although he hardly expected much assistance from Canada, or from the Abolitionists of the North, as Redpath will have it. The arms were evidently especially intended for the slaves, whom he expected to deliver. This is not,

---

[1] Congressional Globe, XXXVI. Cong., 1 Sess., p. 14.
[2] Brown himself says before the court, $250 or $260.

however, by any means equivalent to saying — as not only his enemies but his friends have often asserted — that he intended to excite a universal revolt of the slaves, if the word "revolt" is taken in its usual meaning. During the time Brown was still completely master of the situation, he and his men, when they were asked what they wanted to do, always answered promptly and emphatically, "We want to free the slaves." Brown offered repeatedly to free his prisoners — of whom, for a time, he had about fifty — if he could receive a slave in exchange for each prisoner, and he maintained this declaration unconditionally to the last. And he meant it as he said it. To free the slaves was absolutely his one object. If blood were shed in the attempt, it would be the enemy's fault; liberators and liberated were to make use of their arms only in self-defence. But if any one resisted with violence the freeing of the slaves, he was — according to Brown's view — the attacking party, since the slaves through emancipation merely entered into the enjoyment of their inalienable natural rights. If their would-be owners placed themselves sword in hand between them and their natural rights, then self-defence regardless of consequences was not only a right, but a sacred duty. Yet Brown, as much as any man in the Union, would have shrunk with horror from a massacre of the slaveholders, unless it had been necessary for the liberation of the slaves. But if such an enormous success as Brown dreamed of was at all conceivable, it was only possible in case many thousands of slaves claimed these rights of theirs at the first call of the liberator. And if that happened, was it possible that they should confine themselves to defending these rights, or, rather, was it not certain that they would from the first wade ankle-deep in the blood of their former masters? Any one who had the least acquaintance with the great mass of slaves could not have a moment's doubt as to the answer. But Brown, incredible though it may sound, certainly never even asked himself this question. Nay, more, Brown actually expected that the raid on Harper's Ferry would be the stroke with which Moses called forth water from the rock. The spring was to turn southward, and in its swift course to swell to a mighty river.[1] He declared expressly to Governor Wise, and later still in his letters, that he had not intended simply to break the chains

[1] A map was found among Brown's effects, on which the number of slaves, free colored people, and white people, was carefully marked for each State and county. Evidently his route was to be partially determined by these numbers. It should, however, be mentioned that there were comparatively few slaves in and around Harper's Ferry.

of a few dozen or a few hundred slaves, and to take them again to Canada. Emancipation was to be spread farther and farther, *and the freedmen were to remain in the Southern States.*

Heaven itself could not have brought this about, unless it had sent the angel of judgment to cast down into the dust the whole white population from Florida to Maine. Upon recovering from the stupefaction of the first alarm, the white population of the South would have risen as one man to force the slaves back into the yoke, and the North, with the exception of a handful of the most radical Abolitionists, would have helped the South with all its might. And truly they would have been right; though slavery was an incalculable wrong, though it was an inconceivable curse for the white people, it would have been a still greater misfortune for black and for white, if the former had conquered in a war between the two races. But—aside from this—it was certain that the whole white population would have resolutely taken up the fight, and that the blacks would have been crushed like tinder by their overwhelming force. The more Brown's dreams were realized, the more unavoidable became the conflict between the races; that is, the more did he bring unutterable misery on those he wished to protect. The question of slavery in the United States was a many-sided one, not only from the point of view of expediency, but also from that of morality. In every established law, as such, there is also a moral element. And when it has been possible for an institution such as slavery to remain established law for centuries, then there have been active causes at work which have so broadened and strengthened this moral element that the evil cannot be forcibly overthrown by one blow without deeply wounding relations which morality requires us most scrupulously to respect. And this is my view, although a study of these matters, continued for many years, has persuaded me more and more that the question of slavery in the Union could only be solved by a sharp thrust, dealt by the people themselves, acting under the pressure of an iron necessity. If any one man drew from his catechism the conclusion that he had the moral right to make such an attempt on his own responsibility, then, so far as he succeeded, the number, as well as the importance, of the inevitable immoral consequences must very notably increase.

That in spite of the absolute wickedness of slavery, the slave problem in the United States was even morally a very complicated one, was, and remained to the last, simply incomprehensible to Brown. His reasoning in this matter was made up of two propositions: "Do unto others as you would have them do unto you," and "All men are born free and equal." His sight was keen, but he saw only in a straight line. This is easy to understand when one considers that he looked upon the question only from the ethical point of view. Not only would he have nothing to do with any political party, so that he did not even belong to the Abolitionists, considered as a close organization, but in all the existing sources of information there is not the slightest indication that he ever occupied himself with the question of slavery, considered as a political problem affecting the South, or the North, or the Union as a whole. His position was, however, entirely different as regards the most immediate practical consequences of his undertaking. Although he evidently remained a stranger to the considerations we have just developed, he was certainly able to think coolly and weigh coming events. The irresistible impulse which moved him now at last to do the deed of his life, did not allow him to make use of this power in time, but as soon as he had crossed the Rubicon, his eminently practical instinct, — although perhaps without his being conscious of it — asserted itself fully, and paralyzed his arm. A foreboding came over him that after all he had launched his boat without helm or compass upon a trackless ocean, — that his plan was based on an inherent contradiction, which must necessarily sooner or later cause its failure.

However painful the suggestion may be for those who admire and revere Brown, it sounds like a comic interlude in the tragedy when we read that the man who, against the law of absolute right, against all legal authorities, and against the whole nation, presumed to start a radical, political, and social revolution in the Southern States, which was to be purchased at the cost of a four years' civil war of frightful proportions,— that this man, after the success obtained during the first two hours, remained with folded arms and waited to be hemmed in and hunted down like a mad wolf. But still he stands forth in this hopeless fight, a grand, heroic figure from first to last, while his conquerors have covered themselves with imperishable and absolutely unutterable disgrace and shame. When Brown was completely surrounded, he repeatedly offered to retreat if they would let him take his prisoners along for a short distance as security; after that he was willing, if necessary, to defend his life in open battle. It was entirely in order to reject these conditions. In the eyes of the authorities he was a criminal; they could not embrace his proposition and engage with him in battle according to the rules of chivalry, as though they had stood face to face as individuals possessed of the same rights. But what justification was there for shooting down from a safe cover the men who came out unarmed and under a white flag to escort prisoners? It could not be asserted that they were regarded as poisonous vermin whose extermination by all possible means was a necessity, unless the authors of the statement were willing to accuse themselves of much more cowardly baseness. Brown had quite a number of prisoners. What if he had now said, "an eye for an eye, a tooth for a tooth"? His acting thus would have been conceivable, for it was his own son whom the cowards shot down before his eyes like a mad dog, while he stood unarmed before them. And this was not all, nor was it the worst. William Thompson, Brown's son-in-law, had fallen into the hands of the enemy and had been brought a prisoner to a hotel. A crowd of young heroes were for killing him on the spot. This was with difficulty prevented by a young lady, named Miss Foulke, the sister of the proprietor of the hotel, who threw herself again and again between the prisoner and the revolvers. She is said to have declared later that she did not in the least oppose the execution, she merely did not wish her carpet to be soiled with blood. The carpet was saved from all injury by the heroic girl. Thompson was sent into eternity on the railroad bridge. He fell over the railing and remained lying at the foot of a pillar, but so clumsily had the hangman, who stood close to him, performed his work that he still gave signs of life; a general discharge from the bridge ended his sufferings. Henry Hunter, the son of the prosecuting attorney, boasted before the court that he had played the part of a leader in this heroic deed, and repeatedly declared that he had acted deliberately. Is there any need of saying that he was never in the least troubled by the courts on account of this affair, and that he became one of the lions of the day? And what vengeance did they take, these highway robbers, toward whom the noble Virginians thought every brutal cruelty permissible, if not praiseworthy? Brown had allowed the railroad train to proceed, "in order to reassure those who might have thought we were come here to burn and to kill." He allowed the prisoners to go out with an escort and to reassure their families, and as the firing of the attacking party grew hotter, he warned the prisoners to keep in sheltered corners, that they might not be hurt. One of his sons lay dead at his feet; with his left hand he felt the pulse of his other son, who was dying, while his right hand held his rifle, and his

John Brown.

eye, steady and clear, followed the movements of the enemy. Thus he stood, still warning his surviving companions not to shoot at people who were not engaging in the fight.

The militia had not the courage to seek the lion in his lair. It was not till a body of troops of the United-States marines had come, that an attack on the engine-house was ventured upon. A long ladder did duty as a battering-ram, and the door was broken through at the second onset. All further resistance was now useless. Brown called out to the soldiers who were rushing in that he surrendered. Did they not hear him, or did they shut their ears to his call? At any rate he was lying on the ground without attempting to defend himself when he received several sword-cuts on the head, also bayonet-thrusts in the abdomen. Brown himself, who up to this point had remained unhurt, was generous enough to declare his belief that his being wounded was an unfortunate accident attributable to the confusion of the moment. However, Lieutenant Green acknowledged during Copeland's trial that he had struck Brown on the head after he had already been knocked down, and on being asked again whether Brown was actually lying on the ground, he repeated his statement. At the reproachful request of the prosecuting attorney, Copeland's counsel gave up pushing "such questions" farther.

It is easy to understand why Hunter, the worthy father of a still worthier son, did not like "such questions." But the heroic courage of Brown's conqueror stood out already in such bold relief that it made little difference whether light was thrown on one or the other of the remaining obscure points. I have before me the official report which Colonel Baylor, commander of the militia at Harper's Ferry, made to Governor Wise. From this report[1] I borrow the following facts. Wise's telegrams called into action first of all, I. H. Gibson, who marched at once with the Jefferson Guards and a body of armed citizens of Charlestown from the latter place to Harper's Ferry. At Halltown, halfway between the two points, he telegraphed for immediate reinforcements, to consist of the militia of Frederick County, the Hamtramck Guards, and the Shepherdstown Troop. On reaching Harper's Ferry he was joined by the armed citizens of the place. A few hours later the reinforcements that had been asked for arrived, also a company from Martinsburg, and later in the evening another company from Winchester. Colonel Baylor, who in the mean time

[1] The Life, Trial, and Execution of Capt. John Brown, pp. 40-44.

had assumed the command, summoned in addition the third regiment of cavalry, and formed two more companies of citizens. Before the struggle was over there arrived, besides the Continental Guards under Captain Washington, riflemen under Captain Clarke and three companies from Frederick, Maryland. It would seem that this was a sufficient force against an enemy who had at the first numbered twenty-two men and had in the mean time suffered severe losses. However, when Colonel Lee, who commanded the eighty-five marines, expressed the rash opinion that the militia themselves might have captured the engine-house with its garrison of four combatants, the latter politely declined the honor of making the attack. True, they were not only masters of the art of shooting down prisoners and men under a flag of truce, but fear had taught them the science of multiplication much better than Falstaff had ever learned it. Colonel Baylor tells us that on his arrival the insurgents were estimated at from three hundred to five hundred men.

The Virginians demonstrated amply during the Civil War that they were not cowards. What made them shake in their shoes was not John Brown and his handful of men, but the shadows which their excited imagination saw standing behind them. There is certainly some foundation for the charge that Governor Wise purposely sought to increase the excitement by his extraordinary measures of defence; because he labored under the delusion that this agitation would be an excellent stepping-stone to the presidential chair. But on the whole, neither the fear of shadows nor the excitement was artificially produced. Colonel Baylor declared from the first that the fear lest a rescue could be effected was entirely without foundation.

But the putting under martial law of the whole district around Charlestown, whither the prisoners were brought; the keeping under arms a small army of militia-troops, the sending of fresh troops and artillery to Charlestown by Governor Wise on the first false alarm, and his praising the soldiers for not looking "pale with fear;" the not even allowing John Brown's wife to approach the prison except under a strong military escort; the chaining of the wounded man, who was unable to stand, to a fellow-prisoner, and the bringing him to his first hearing under a guard of eighty men; the glittering of bayonets all over the court-house; finally, the assumption by the State of the control of the railroads shortly before the execution, for greater security, and the introduction of a strict system of passports, — all this was to a great extent a wretched humbug gotten up for effect. There were plenty of people in the South

John Brown.

who were fully conscious of this. The "Charleston Mercury," the most influential organ of the extremists, called it, "The Virginia Farce and its Terrorism,—a tissue of the most disgraceful exaggeration and invention, such as must excite the gall of every Southerner who has regard for the dignity and personal responsibility of the Southern people." The same sheet declared: "It seems really as though the men who hold the telegraph wires had joined together to make us an object of mockery and ridicule to ourselves and to the world."[1] Yet it was no humbug, but a genuine scare, which drove couriers to horse, and set the telegraph in motion for every burning haystack, and brought a poor cow to its death because it ventured to approach the sentinels without knowing the watchword. When, later on, the representatives of Virginia complained bitterly

[1] Congressional Globe, *loc. cit.*, p. 65.

in the Senate that the North had shown so little sympathy for Virginia in its misfortune and distress, Chandler replied: "We do not understand a case like this. . . . If seventeen or twenty-two generals from Virginia and North Carolina were to attack Springfield, I will guarantee that, supposing there were not a man within five thousand miles, the women would bind them fast within thirty minutes, and would not demand any sympathy. . . . The papers tell us that Governor Wise compared the population of Harper's Ferry to sheep. That is slanderous; it is not true, for I have never yet seen a flock of fifty or one hundred sheep in which there was not one warlike bell-wether!"[1] Cutting words, but true. How could the North understand that a town of three thousand (others say five thousand) inhabitants in a great State like Virginia could be driven into a panic

[1] *Congressional Globe, loc. cit.*, p. 34.

by a body of twenty-two men? But the fact that such things were possible in the South was not lost on the North. The stunning effect which this raid produced on the South gave the lie in the most emphatic and annihilating fashion to the insolent and insane hymns which were being constantly sung in praise of slavery. If his deed had produced no other effect, Brown would still have been justified in his glorious declaration that he willingly mounted the scaffold, since his life and that of his fellows had not been offered up in vain to the great cause.

The best evidence of the frightful genuineness of the panic is the brazen impudence with which it was brought forward as the justifying motive for the many atrocities which marked the trial. The brutalizing influences of slavery came to light with terrible vividness. Kapp's statement that Brown "enjoyed very careful treatment" is not mistaken, but it is true only of the later period of his imprisonment. Watson Brown, whose life was prolonged until the early morning of the 19th of October, complained of the hard bench he was forced to lie on. His fellow-prisoner, Coppoc, begged for a mattress, or at least a blanket, for the dying man, but could obtain neither. Both Brown himself and Stevens, who was even more seriously wounded, had nothing furnished them but wretched straw. Redpath (p. 373) assures us that "from October 19 till November 7 no clean clothing was given to Brown, but that he lay in his soiled and blood-stained garments just as he had fallen at Harper's Ferry." On the 25th of October he was brought before the court; he was not at first carried there on a camp-bed, as was the case afterward, but compelled to walk, leaning on two men. Virginia could not wait till he could stand. And why was

Virginia in so much haste? Hunter said the expenses were too large; the judges declared that the term would soon be over, and they wished to dispose of the cases against the leaders before the end, and Hunter crowned the whole matter by demanding that Virginia should be released from her anxiety. Brown cost Virginia dear indeed. The commissioners to whom the financial side of the business was intrusted handed in to the State an account of $185,667.03.[1] But it was certainly gloriously original to make a state trial an extremely costly amusement by means of the wildest and most useless precautionary measures while the prosecuting attorney was continually crying out, "Hurry him to the gallows, or the taxpayers will be making wry faces at us." Why should the prosecuting attorney not bring forward such reasons, however, if the

[1] The Independent, March 8, 1860.

judges did not make it their sole and only care to pronounce righteously and to guard most carefully the rights which humanity and the laws emphatically accord to the man who is tried for his life? And if the judges wanted above all things to get through, why should the prosecuting attorney blush for shame as he stated that the defendants must be delivered over to the executioner as soon as possible, because "there can be no woman in the whole county who, with or without reason, does not tremble with anxiety and fear" as long as a half-dozen of prisoners, most of them severely wounded, have not been sent to their last account?

A dreadful picture is here!—a courthouse, in front of which cannon have been dragged, and which is packed with people who do not wish to hear a verdict but a condemnation; the condemnation of a man of sixty years who lies covered with wounds on his litter, manifesting a marvellous composure, listening without the least excitement to attorney and judges as they heartily unite in the decision that all possible means must be employed for hastening his fearful end. When the hearing revealed the story of Thompson's cruel fate in all its particulars, the tears rolled down Brown's cheeks, but the gallows erected for himself was in his eyes a ladder to heaven, and he greeted it with a smile. It was only his sense of justice and the wish not to let the motives of his action be covered over with foul, mendacious mud, which made him demand what he would have obtained as a matter of course in every State where the laws are properly administered. On his very first appearance in court, Brown begged the judges for their own sakes and for his not to give him a sham trial. "When I was taken prisoner," said he, " I did not ask for quarter; I did not ask that my life be spared. The governor of Virginia assured me that I should have a fair trial, but under no circumstances shall I be able to secure one. If you want my blood, you can have it at any moment without going through with this mockery of a trial. I have had no lawyer. I have been unable to take advice of any one.... There are extenuating circumstances which I would adduce in our favor, if we could be granted a fair hearing. But if you wish to force an empty form upon us — a trial for the purpose of hanging us — you had better spare your pains. I am ready to meet my fate."[1]

The court's answer proved that he was indeed to have a trial only "for the purpose of hanging him." Brown asked for a short postponement until he should be in a little better state of health. He

[1] The Life, Trial, and Execution of Capt. John Brown, p. 55.

could not now, he said, rely upon his memory, and his hearing was for the time being still so much affected by the scalp-wounds he had received that he could not understand what was said. The prosecuting attorney requested the court not to take notice of these "trifling statements." As the physician's opinion agreed with Hunter's wishes, the court maintained that it was entirely in order to bring before its bar on a camp-bed a man suffering from five serious wounds — one of his kidneys had been pricked or cut into — on trial for his life. Brown had moreover requested a delay of two or three days to give time for the arrival of the lawyer whom he had asked to undertake his defence. His request was denied; the court assigned him two lawyers; and the trial began before Brown had been able to speak a word to the counsel that had been given him. Brown was right; a fair trial was out of the question from the outset, for in no slave State, and least of all in Virginia, could a jury be brought together in the usual way which would not come with preconceived opinions, such as would make a condemnation absolutely sure. But when we consider that in addition to a court of slave-holders and a jury as above described, there were assigned as counsel for the defence, lawyers who were also born and bred under the poisonous breath of slavery, we perceive that it was an insult to talk of a fair trial, however honorable the judges, jurymen, and lawyers might be. And moreover, it was an outrage, under the existing circumstances, to deny the defendant, whose life was at stake, a delay of two days in order that he might secure the counsel he wanted.

It has been said, in order to justify the refusal of the court, that they acted in the belief that Brown only wished for a postponement in order to improve his chances of being forcibly rescued. One might almost be tempted at first sight to believe that such fears were genuinely entertained when one reads at the end of one of the official reports, "The jailers have orders to shoot down all the prisoners, if an attempt is made to deliver them." But this excuse can hardly stand when we consider the decision which forbade all exhaustive reports of the trial, and the refusal to allow reporters access to Brown, — a refusal which was explained by some one of the slave-holders' party to have been due to the fear that he might say something calculated to influence public opinion, and to have a bad effect on the slaves."[1] But even if the members of the court really believed at first that Brown wished to protect himself by means of

[1] The Life, Trial, and Execution of Capt. John Brown, pp. 57, 58.

empty pretexts, they speedily received the proof that this assumption was entirely false. His counsel submitted a paper to the court, which, pointing to the fact that several of the members of Brown's family had been or were still insane, suggested that a mental derangement might be assumed in his case also. The facts were correct, and Brown might therefore have obtained a much longer postponement; but he repelled "with scorn," as a very poor device, the insinuation that he was not in his senses. Now what did the court do, when, as frequently happened, a postponement of a day or of a few hours was again requested? With one exception the request was denied, and in this one instance Hunter expressly protested against its being granted. And yet it was a question of waiting for the arrival of lawyers from the free States, who had telegraphed that they were coming, or of allowing Hoyt a few hours' rest before beginning the defence, — Hoyt was a young lawyer from Massachusetts who had worked all night, straining his powers to the utmost, in order to gain in haste some knowledge of the statutes of Virginia bearing on the case, but had not yet been able to read through the testimony of the witnesses who had been examined before his arrival, and was completely exhausted in body and mind. Toward the end the defendant's lawyers were even obliged to haggle with the court over the number of hours within which they were to confine their concluding speeches.

Still further evidence of Brown's magnanimity is furnished by his statement that the trial was conducted as fairly as could have been expected under the circumstances. Nor do I myself mean to say that the verdict would or could have been otherwise than it was. I do not believe it would, although it is possible to raise quite a number of objections — which can be supported by extracts from the constitutional and from the criminal law — against the drawing up of the suit and consequently against the judgment rendered. However, these are merely technical legal points, and the trial was eminently a political one. Forms were sinned against, but in the main, justice was done. He who undertakes such a game stakes his life. Brown had forfeited his life, and that not only according to the laws of Virginia, for in every State where the death penalty exists he would necessarily have been condemned for a similar crime. The motives which actuated him must furnish the ground on which to judge his character, but the jury and the court in rendering judgment could only deal with the facts.

There was no such haste to carry out

the sentence as there had been to bring the trial to a close. On the 2d of November, Brown was sentenced to suffer death by hanging on the 2d of December. Several thousand militia-men, infantry, and cavalry, had been called out for the day, and loaded cannon had been posted so as to command the gallows and the streets, as though it were very much to be feared that Brown would be rescued at the last moment from the hands of the executioner; and yet no stranger was allowed to come within two or three miles of the place of execution. One cannot wonder at this, since even the would-be spectators from the neighborhood were kept so far from the gallows that Brown's voice could not have reached them; and yet there was certainly not one among them who would have raised his finger to keep the rope from Brown's throat. During the previous days they had glutted their eyes gazing on the fatal rope, which was publicly exposed. It is characteristic of the feeling in the South that three States contended for the honor of furnishing this rope. Kapp, however, is wrong when he says, in accordance with the first newspaper reports, that South Carolina carried the day in this noble contest. The cotton of the plantation State was too weak to bear John Brown's weight. The preference had to be given to hemp, which grows in more northern climes, and the hemp used had been grown in Henry Clay's State, — the border State of Kentucky.[1] There was a fitness in this. The North and South were equally responsible for the hanging of John Brown.

Brown was writing his will up to the last moment. When the parting came, he exhorted his companions, heartily, to be firm, and gave each of them — with the

[1] The Independent, Dec. 8, 1859.

exception of Cook, who had attempted to buy his life by falsehoods — twenty-five cents, "since he had no more use for money." Thus is his ideal childish simplicity carried to almost inconceivable lengths; and yet he does not for one moment cease to be a thoroughly sober, practical American. In speaking of the bringing up of his daughters, he exhorts his wife not to forget that "the music of the broom and the wash-tub, of the needle and the spinning-wheel, of the sickle and the flail," should precede that of the piano; and in one of his last letters he complains that she has not told him anything of the condition of the crops on the little farm. The often-repeated story that on coming out of prison he took a negro woman's child from her arms and kissed it, is presumably a poetic embellishment. I do not find the circumstance mentioned in the most reliable reports that I am acquainted with, and considering the exaggerated precautions which were taken, it is not likely that negroes were allowed to come near him. Moreover, anything that would have looked like a scene out of a play was repugnant to his nature. The crystal-clear truthfulness of his nature is illustrated once more by the fact that he remained perfectly simple and natural up to the last. On being asked whether he considers himself an instrument in the hands of Providence, he answers simply and firmly, "I do." True, he declares that he is not being executed but "publicly murdered," and yet not for a single minute does he attempt to clothe himself with the air of a martyr and saint. Sitting on his own coffin, he takes his last journey; but he lets his eye wander over the sunny landscape with quiet earnestness, as though he were looking with a friend at his own

North Elba, and says, "This is a beautiful country." With a firm step he mounts the ladder leading up to the gallows. On the sheriff's handing him a cloth to give the signal when he shall be ready, he refuses it, and says, "I am ready at any time, but do not make me wait longer than is necessary." This last request was not fulfilled. The sheriff received orders to wait, and the troops began to go through all sorts of evolutions. Brown had to wait ten minutes with the cap drawn over his eyes and with his hands bound. He stood erect, without shuddering in the least, or betraying any excitement. The undertaker had said to him during the ride, "Captain Brown, you are in better spirits to-day than I;" and he had answered, "I have good cause to be so." When the sheriff, indignant at General Taliaferro's cruelty, asked him pityingly if he were not tired, he answered,

"Not tired; but don't make me wait any longer than is absolutely necessary." These were his last words.

This closing scene of the tragedy filled the North with horror. People said and rightly too, that such things could not have happened north of Mason and Dixon's line at the execution of the most abject criminal. Yet individuals might be directly responsible for these barbarities, while the fact itself of Brown's execution would have to be settled by every one with the whole South and with himself. The President's way of doing this was to give a dinner to the diplomatic corps on the day of the execution. This was a method which did not accord with the feelings of either party. There were certainly many men among the Southern aristocracy who perceived the want of tact of any demonstration on the part of the federal executive, nor was such a petty and underhand proceeding calculated to please any Southern "fire-eater." But the North looked upon Brown with a feeling which turned Buchanan's dinner into a cowardly, contemptible insult. A few only called the execution a piece of meanness, but thousands and ten thousands who unreservedly acknowledged that death by the hand of the executioner was the legitimate result of his undertaking honored his memory by solemn religious ceremonies. "What sort of a system is this, which drives men like Brown to acts rendering a resort to the executioner's axe a horrible but unavoidable necessity?" This was the question that lay on countless lips, and it was a question of immense importance. Pitiful though the attitude of most politicians was toward this affair, — the Democrats seeking with greedy eagerness to make it a poisonous arrow in the flesh of the Republicans, and the Republicans repelling with holy horror as a shameful calumny the charge that they were not filled with as great an aversion toward the deed as the most conscientious Democrat, — the best portion of the people in all classes were pervaded and thrilled by the conviction that a martyr had laid down his life as an offering for the sins of the nation, and that the fateful, "All ready, Mr. Sheriff," on the field of Charlestown, was not the end of the matter; this seed sown in blood must needs bring forth a mighty harvest, — it must become a curse or a blessing.

People were far from looking upon Brown in this light from the first. The "New York Tribune," in many respects the most prominent and most extreme organ of the Republicans, summed up the case by calling him simply "a madman;" and the "Independent," one of the most radical anti-slavery papers outside of the small circle of Abolitionists in the narrowest sense of the word, described him on the 20th of October as "a lawless brigand." On November 24, on the other hand, the "Independent" declares, "The people's verdict has already stamped John Brown as a brave and honest man." And on December 8, the same sheet writes: "No man has ever made such a profound impression on this nation through his moral heroism. . . . Each of his actions, each word he spoke up to the time of his execution has only strengthened and increased the power of his example. He grew constantly greater up to the end. He was greatest at the last, when most men would have been weakest." Here we have an example of the change of opinion concerning Brown which took place during his six weeks' imprisonment, and he who carefully follows his intellectual and spiritual life during this period will fully understand this change. When a slave-holder said to him in prison, "You are a fanatic," he answers with the quiet of conviction, "You yourself are a fanatic." And before the court he declares, "I consider it not unlawful, but lawful that I have thus taken the place of God's despised arm. If it is thought right that I should lose my life to further the purposes of righteousness, and to mingle my blood with that of my children and with that of the millions of slaves in this land whose rights have been trodden down by sinful, cruel, and unrighteous laws, why, then, be it so." Here John Brown takes his stand; every word and action afford fresh evidence that this and this alone is the ground on which his feet rest. Even in the smallest things he remains true to himself. He goes steadfastly and evenly on his way, even to the dark end, as though an irresistible natural law were driving him on. The number of his letters written in prison is considerable, and not even in the most confidential of these can the closest scrutiny discover the faintest tinge of selfishness. "To me all is joy;" the Bible words are the dominant note, which rings full and clear through all his utterances concerning himself. When his family had been cared for and the education of his minor children secured by means of collections at the North, the one shadow departed from his soul. But even this anxiety never drew from him a sickly, sentimental word, and its removal does not cause his imagination to soar even an inch above the sober ground of reality. He writes to his wife, "Helping poor widows and their children is not much more romantic than trying to help poor negroes." He is — I repeat it — no enthusiast, no fanatic in the common acceptation of the term; and it is precisely for this reason that his character makes so powerful an impression. There is no gloss about him; he is all substance. His terrible earnestness compels people in spite of themselves to believe in his moral greatness, and the touching moderation with which he gives his executioners, considered simply as men, more than their due, takes away the repellant effect of the one-sided roughness and rigidity of his moral convictions. He gave the highest proof a man can give of the genuineness of these convictions; for their sake he staked his life and that of his children, without the possibility of any selfish advantage, and when he lost, he did not regret what he had done. "Time and the honest verdict of posterity," said he, "will justify all my actions." Millions of eyes were fastened upon him in anxious expectation, to see whether he would not betray at the last moment that he was wearing a mask, even though this mask might be woven of the thinnest gauze wire. But after he had stood ten minutes like a statue with the rope round his neck and the cap drawn over his eyes, the millions drew a deep breath, — he was wholly pure, wholly true. And this is why John Brown's life and death struck the minds and consciences of the North with a far mightier blow than the Lundys, Garrisons, and Douglases could deal with their most heartfelt speeches.

Brown recognized fully the magnitude of the impression which he and his deed made on the North, and it was through this impression that he for the first time fully appreciated what he had done. He did not perceive that his undertaking could not have succeeded under any circumstances; but he did see that his failure and its consequences achieved much greater results than its most complete success could have done. His acknowledgment that he had been led by God in the best way when he delivered himself through his own folly into the hands of his enemies was not merely owing to his Christian faith, but to a clear insight into the facts. "I can leave to God," he writes, "the time and manner of my death, for I believe now that the sealing of my testimony before God and man with my blood will do far more to further the cause to which I have earnestly devoted myself, than anything else I have done in my life." And a few days later, "My health improves slowly, and I am quite cheerful concerning my approaching end, since I am convinced that I am worth infinitely more on the gallows than I could be anywhere else."

The most intelligent men of the South can hardly have failed to recognize the truth of this assertion. The rumor that Governor Wise would pardon Brown if he dared to follow his personal inclination was perhaps not entirely unfounded.[1] Not all intelligent and cultivated people are so high-minded when they recognize the noble qualities of an enemy as to take pains to acknowledge them. It is easy to understand that even such men as Senator Mason could not refrain from characterizing Brown by the epithets, "rough," "thief," "highwayman," and "wretched vagabond." Governor Wise, however, honored himself by giving Brown the character of a man of extraordinary fearlessness, truth, and fidelity to principle. And this view of Brown's character, as a serious warning for the South, was confirmed so emphatically by a number of fanatical slave-holders, that only half of the wild abuse of the majority can be considered genuine; the other half was partly political manœuvring, partly the hissing of powerless rage. How much would these gentlemen have given to suc-

[1] Washington letter of Nov. 5 to the "Independent."

ceed in their attempt to point out a direct complicity on the part of prominent Republicans, or to have proved that Brown was merely the weak-headed tool of some other man, who, safe in his own house, indulged in the pleasure of being fanatical! It seemed to them a sacred, patriotic duty to tear down Brown's character; they understood very well how essential it was for the political side of the question to consider the motives which actuated him, though they had been of no use to him in court. How often they had scornfully called on the Abolitionists to turn their words into action for once, and to come to the South, where the ropes were already twisted for them! Now one of them had come and had substantiated his doctrine by reckless action, and he had not even blinked at the sight of the rope. Thousands who till then had been unwilling to believe it were now convinced of the genuineness of the moral sentiment of the North in regard to slavery, though they still stoutly denied the fact. Not that they had really believed the North to be swarming with John Browns. But a generation had not yet gone by since Garrison had been dragged through the streets of Boston with a rope round his neck, and the houses of the philanthropic Tappans had been pulled down in New York because they declared that every compromise with slavery was a chimera and a monstrosity. And this short space of time had not only given birth successively to the Freedom, Free-Soil and Republican parties, but the Democratic party at the North had been split and its foundations shaken by the agitation connected with slavery. Those were signs of the times which the Southerners had not passed by unheeding. But John Brown first revealed to them the full meaning of Calhoun's declaration that the spirit of abolitionism unless its germ were destroyed could never be suppressed, because it was able to control the pulpit and the school, and that it would infallibly break up the Union, because it was a religious conviction. Now they only hoped against their own conviction that the stream would still be arrested in its course. When a boat at the crossing of the stream above Niagara Falls is turned out of its course, every stroke of the oars is watched anxiously from both shores. As the prow of the boat turns toward the middle of the river, cheeks grow pale, but there is still hope, for the oars strike the waters with twofold energy. When the rapids have been reached, the gazers hold their breath, for there is only one chance of rescue: the boatman may succeed in casting himself on one of the small islands. But when the force of the current has driven him beyond them, then eyes are closed, and hearts filled with horror exclaim, "God have mercy on his soul!" For seventy years the politicians had been trying in vain to struggle with the boat of the slavery question against the mighty stream of actual facts and against the moral principles which were operating among these facts. The boat had been constantly driven farther and farther down stream, but hope had as yet never been utterly given up, though fear had often gotten the upper hand. But now John Brown, in the grim earnestness of his religious convictions, had put his foot on the boat as it was drifting in the rapids and given it a mighty shove away from the shore of the last island. True, he was the first to fall overboard and to be hurried to the depths below. But was there now any chance that the leaky skiff should not follow him over the Falls? At last it dawned on the people that even supposing none but Henry Clays to sit in the councils of the nation, the time must come when it would be absolutely impossible to throw a new bridge of compromise across the chasm which had been opened between North and South by the contradictory principles embodied in the Constitution. Brown's execution sealed the irrepressibleness of the conflict between North and South.

Kapp concludes his estimate of Brown with the words, " Vivat sequens." This conclusion has been deprecated by people who have a right to express an opinion on American affairs. To me it has no hard or painful sound. The sentence is the victorious battle shout of a man who stands in the midst of the fray. But a battle shout was justified, and the joy of victory from which it sprang is like the breath of fresh morning air after a sultry night of storm. There were still many of whom it could be said in the words of the Bible, "They call out, peace, peace!" but they too received the answer, "And yet there is no peace!" The era of constant terror was past. On November 24 the "Independent" wrote: "What is it that will be hanged on the gallows before the eyes of all men? Not John Brown, but slavery. . . . John Brown swinging on the gallows will ring the knell of slavery." The frightful end was close at hand from which a new and better future was to be born. One year after the execution of Brown, on the 20th of December, 1860, South Carolina declared its secession from the Union, and on May 11, 1861, the Second Massachusetts Regiment of infantry was raised, which was first to sing on its march South, —

"John Brown's body lies mouldering in the grave,
His soul goes marching on."

H. VON HOLST.

THE FLOODS,

A POEM BY D. A. WASSON.

THE FLOODS.

IN MEMORY OF JOHN BROWN.

BY D. A. WASSON.

LOOK how a river, brimmed, then heaped
    yet more,
  Will drown his banks, and flood the regions
    nigh,
Spreading with bounty terrible, the store
  Of melting mountain and dissolving sky.

So may a soul of power, an Amazon
  Of heavenly purpose, — being o'ergraced with
    good, —
Break from the banks of prudence, rolling on
  A kingdom's quiet his aggression rude.

And as before the unappeasèd urge
  Of influence hurrying from the heart of heaven,

He rises, widens 'yond all wonted verge —
  Still on — o'er hold and hearth of Custom
    driven,

We that, mayhap, see Order in the guise
  Of our own safety only, cry, " Behold,
These forces rude the name of Law despise;
  They mock it in their foray fierce and bold."

Hidden from timid eyes the truth will be!
  For, lo! the deluge, too, is Order's child;
Its waters hasten but from sky to sea;
  And though we citizens may deem them wild,

They journey as they must, — while straying, still
  Chasing their lawful channel where it goes,
Nor wid'ning but by affluence of that Will
  Which out of heaven beyond containing flows.

And when at length their swelling tides are gone
  The plain lies higher, and the fertile shore
Is farther stretched by that alluvion
  Whose wealth the deluge in its bosom bore.

The Floods.

Oh, from earth's history were the floods away,
  Not well had ripened here the cosmic plan!
For many a happy harvester to-day
  Gathers in golden corn their gifts to man.

And from the record of man's deed and thought
  Were razèd out that deluge-height of soul
Which makes the fountained bosom all too fraught
  To yield effect by nice and legal dole,

Sure, men would hiss their drawling destinies,
  And hist'ry creep, as 't were, through cowherd lanes.
Deep ran the plough where high the harvest is;
  The man-child breathes but by a mother's pains.

APPENDIX.

APPENDIX.

THE BUST OF JOHN BROWN.

THE effect of momentous events on light-minded persons is often very slight; but on serious men they leave an indelible impression, which usually shows itself in the aspect of the face. Especially do wounds and suffering deepen the expression of the countenance, and bring out the features in a strong and pure relief. Mr. E. A. Brackett, when he returned from Charlestown, Va., in November, 1859, said to the lady who had commissioned him to make a marble bust of John Brown : "You have never seen John Brown! I mean that no one who has not seen him in prison can be said to have seen him at his very best. He is glorious to look upon!" It was under this impression that the sculptor began his work, and in a short time produced a work of art which in conception at least might compare well with any of the heads of Greek divinities, though, like all modern work, it falls far short of them in execution. It is too narrow to be purely Greek, and this peculiarity, which is more noticeable in the photograph than in the bust itself, cannot be wholly accounted for on the ground that Brown was a native of New England. The sculptor, however, has been most fortunate in moulding a face in which strong Roman-like features are united with perfect classic repose. The eyes have an expression as if looking into the far distance, as we look at clouds beyond the horizon. The lines about the mouth resemble those on the Zeus which is attributed to Phidias. These lines are rarely seen in real life, but they can be noticed in all the pictures of John Brown, and are no invention of the artist. It seems as if thus Constantine must have looked, and the great Christian emperors, of whose appearance we have no good record, for Greek art had died out before their time. It must have been the pose of the head and the aspect of great moral force which led Sumner to compare it to Michelangelo's Moses, for otherwise there is no resemblance. Neither does it resemble decidedly any other work in marble that I have anywhere seen. It is somewhat idealized, — for how otherwise can the spirit of man be represented in cold marble? — but not too much so. Compared in this respect with Crawford's Beethoven, it is a realistic likeness. Mr. Brackett writes, " As to the bust of John Brown, I can only say that I intended it as a physical and mental *likeness of the man*. Your father, Wendell Phillips, and Dr. S. G. Howe expressed their entire approbation of it as a likeness." It was at first placed on exhibition among the busts of the Roman emperors in the Boston Athenæum, and Mrs. Brown, coming upon it there without previous intimation, recognized it and wept. Idealized or not, it represents John Brown much better than the pictures which are current of him, designed from bad photographs or daguerreotypes. There are peculiarities of light and perspective in photography which make its results always uncertain and in many cases quite unreliable. The best photographs are always in slight variation from their subjects, and bad ones are only better than no pictures at all. Mont Blanc as seen from the Mauvais Pas is a sky-piercing dome, but in a photograph taken from the same point of view it appears as a spot of light too small to attract attention. Every one must have felt the mental shock which arises from the first look at the photograph of an intimate friend. John Brown himself had a stern but friendly and attractive countenance; ladies admired him, and little children went to him, which they would hardly have done had he looked as most of these pictures represent him.

THE JOHN BROWN MEDAL.

THIS medal has finally been deposited by Mrs. Brown in the museum of the Kansas State Historical Society at Topeka. In 1870 a committee of leading French philanthropists was appointed at a meeting held in Paris to superintend the construction of a handsome gold medal in honor of the martyr of Harper's Ferry. Such, however, was the confusion which ensued upon the Franco-German war that the plan was not carried out until 1874, in the autumn of which year it was received by Mrs. Brown at North Elba, N. Y. The following letter accompanied it : —

(*Translation.*)

PARIS, Oct. 21, 1874.

TO MADAME, WIDOW OF JOHN BROWN.

MADAME, — Many years have passed away since the day when your noble husband completed the sacrifice of a life devoted to the most benevolent of causes. From the gallows where he was hung has gone forth this cry of universal indignation, which has been the signal for the complete deliverance of a disinherited race. Honor to him and his worthy sons, together with his widow! To the benedictions with which the present century follows their memory those of future centuries will be added. Such thoughts must produce, Madame, a great alleviation of your grief; but you have claimed the best compensation for your afflictions from this superior mandate, that above the poor justice of men soars the supreme justice, which leaves no good action without its recompense, neither any crime without punishment. You will also receive, we hope, with a feeling of solace this witness of the sympathy of the French republicans, the expression of which would have arrived less tardily but for the long and cruel ordeals through which our unfortunate country has just passed.

We beg you, Madame, to accept the homage of our profound respect.

In the name of all their colleagues the undersigned members of the committee on subscription.

VICTOR HUGO,	PATRICE LARROQUE,
ÉTIENNE ARAGO,	LOUIS BLANC,
CAPRON,	CH. L. CHASSIN,
MELVIL BLONCOURT,	LAURENT PICHAT,
EUGÈNE PELLETON,	V. SCHOELCHER,

L. GORNET.

Appendix. 191

Certainly the French hold the first place among nations in their sympathy and encouragement for struggling humanity. Among the names of this committee Victor Hugo and Louis Blanc alone are popularly known in this country, but the others are also distinguished in France, as distinguished and respectable as the names of William M. Evarts, John A. Lowell, or George W. Childs are on the Atlantic seaboard.

Étienne Arago, born at Perpignan, 1802, not the astronomer, but a littérateur who has written a great many light comedies. He is also a republican politician of decidedly radical tendencies, and was mayor of Paris during the siege in 1870. He is not a communist, however, and has since retired from politics.

Victor Schoelcher, born at Paris, 1804, a distinguished writer and politician who has written much on the subject of slavery. His first pamphlet appeared in 1833, with the title, "De l' des Noirs et de la Législation Coloniale;" and he presided over the commission which drew up the statute abolishing slavery in the French colonies April 27, 1848. He was representative in the Chamber of Deputies from 1848 to 1851, and after having been exiled during the reign of Napoleon III., was again from 1871 to 1875, when he was chosen a life member of the French Senate, — most surely a remarkable and highly honorable career.

Patrice Larroque was born at Beauve, Côte d'Or, March 27, 1801, and died in Paris in 1879. He was a professor of philosophy, and has written mostly on philosophical and religious subjects. One of his books, "De l'Esclavage chez les patrons Chrétiennes," published in 1857, proves him to have been an Abolitionist.

Eugène Pelleton, born Oct. 29, 1813, at Saint-Palais-sur-Mer, was in early life a journalist and author of somewhat mystical turn of mind, and wrote for a variety of newspapers. After 1863 he became a politician, and during the war of 1870 he was a member of the Government of National Defence, and since then he has been a member of the Senate. He is a moderate republican.

Melvil Bloncourt was born at Point-à-Pitre, in

Appendix. 193

the French West Indies, Oct. 23, 1825, a lawyer, journalist, author, and politician of radical and socialistic views. He was an important official during the Paris commune, and was in 1874 condemned to death for it by court martial. He had already taken French leave, however, and has since been living in Switzerland. Probably his character was not as well known at the time this committee was organized as it now is.

Charles L. Chassin, born at Nantes, Feb. 11, 1831, journalist and littérateur, and in politics a moderate republican.

Laurent Pichat, born in Paris, 1823, is a poet, a politician of the advanced republican type, and a friend of Victor Hugo's. He is now a senator for life.

Louis Blanc, born at Madrid, in 1813, was a journalist, historian, and prominent political agitator in 1848. His exposure of the corrupt methods of the government of Louis Philippe are supposed to have contributed largely to its overthrow; but the failure of his impracticable socialistic schemes also contributed to the overthrow of the revolutionary government in whose counsels he had too much influence. He lived in exile during the whole period of the second empire, but returned to France in 1871, and was chosen a member of the national assembly. Although a *visionary thinker* and a *prejudiced writer*, the uprightness of his life and purity of his motives have caused Louis Blanc to be respected by fair-minded men of all political parties. He took no part in the Paris commune of 1871, and his socialistic doctrines are of so mild and peaceable a type that he would seem to be as far removed from the anarchist of to-day on the one hand as from the Bonapartes on the other. That pure-minded but impractical dreamers often do mischief in the world of realities is only too true, but whether they are to be blamed for it is another question.

Among this brilliant company of gifted and venerable men Melvil Bloncourt is the only name which seems to be in some degree unworthy of the rest. Is there not commonly a Judas among every twelve men? Anarchists and socialists attach themselves to John Brown

Appendix.

as barnacles do to a whale, or as the most eccentric forms of woman's rights, teetotalism, and spiritism formerly attached themselves to the early Abolitionists. Those who go through life with such a veneration for form as never to see the inside of anything may readily confound John Brown with the anarchists, simply because *the actions* of the former were equally revolutionary with the *principles* of the other; but this is no less a blunder than it would be to mistake the moon for the sun because both are round and of about the same size. John Brown made war upon a concrete case of political injustice, but the anarchists set themselves against all abstract political right. The one could not even serve as an illustration of the other, even if reasoning by comparison were not the most fallacious form of logic. The anarchists might indeed learn from the example of John Brown's life such contentment in poverty, such disinterested pursuit of a lofty ideal, and such reverence for the unseen spirit which is above man, as might be the proper corrective for their envious and materialistic theories. The salutary discipline of John Brown's camp in Kansas, with prayers morning and evening, might have benefited their moral good health, as it is supposed to have the captured border ruffians. The anarchists do not draw their mental sustenance from John Brown's life and principles, but as Mr. William M. Salter has clearly demonstrated in a dissertation on the subject, from certain English and French writers on political economy, the most materialistic of all sciences that have as yet been discovered. The feudal system of mediæval Europe is the only form of socialism which has ever proved successful, and it is probable that if socialism should ever become paramount it would again revert after a series of changes to a similar form.

LETTER

TO A LADY PATIENT TO WHOM WAS PROMISED AN ACCOUNT OF A VISIT TO JOHN BROWN'S GRAVE.

SARANAC LAKES, July 27, 1865.

DEAR MRS. H——,

I promised to write to you from John Brown's grave. I thought while there of my promise; but as I had only a short time to stay, and many people were visiting the spot, I have postponed writing to you until now.

I am at Bartlett's, — the prince of hosts in these mountain regions, — who, living here many years with his charming and energetic, warm-hearted wife, makes a sort of paradise for lovers of angling and shooting, or still larger numbers of devotees to eating delicious trout or sweet, tender venison-steaks. In this little *bijou* of a hotel, and with the sound of rushing waterfalls in my ears, within close view of the eternal hills, and while breathing the clear, cool air of heaven, I redeem my pledge.

I stood by the side of John Brown's grave yesterday.

He was, or rather he is now, one of my God-sent heroes,— a man specially allowed to appear at the appointed hour with a sort of John the Baptist mission, and who sealed that mission with his blood. I thought his design foolish and wrong; and how foolish was *my* thought as I consider subsequent events, which made him the leader of our hosts in the Civil War, during which "his soul was marching on," and compelled even his enemies to admire him even while they sought his life.

While I think now of his quiet self-possession in prison; his brave words to his companions just before his death; his admiration of the beauty of Nature while going toward the place of execution; his thanks to his jailer and others for acts of kindness; his walk, firm and elastic, up the scaffold-step; his gentleness and yet his perfect manliness even to the last,— my reverence for him exceeds, far exceeds, the reverence I have for any other being save Christ, or Socrates while drinking the hemlock. And how ennobling is such an example as Brown's to all the race! Knowing him to be mortal like ourselves, we for a time at least understand the fine expression made use of by Dr. James Walker in one of his sermons: "There is the power of an archangel locked up in the breast of every man, and a sufficient motive only is needed to bring it forth."

But a truce to all my musings! You want me to redeem my promise and to describe his tomb. Most fitting is the spot; nothing could be finer.

It had been raining all night, and the morning was showery when we started from Lower Jay, a small village in the town of North Elba, in New York. We soon struck off from the main road, through a huge swinging gate, and driving along through a field of grass, soon entered a primeval forest. "The corpses of great old trees," as Holmes, I believe, has it, lay at the feet of splendid tall oaks and delicately fringed larches or rugged wide-branching pines. The leaves glittered in the morning sunlight, and the air was sweet as honey to the lips; the song of birds was in our ears. The road, a simple by-path for our wheels, meandered up hill and down for nearly three quarters of a mile, when suddenly we emerged into a magnificent "clearing" of many hundred acres, lying broadly embosomed in an amphitheatre of mountains. The clouds, which had been lowering all the morning, lifted themselves from the summits of many of the higher peaks, and some of the clouds became so fleecy over them as to let us see the morning sun playing up over their loftiest points. The scene was grand in the extreme. A finer spot for the tomb of a pious and brave man could not have been selected; and I could not help feeling how much the martyr must have gained in strength from his very residence. "I will lift up mine eyes unto the hills, whence cometh my strength." I am sure that often to his genuinely pious soul, a lover of the Bible, the whole of this noble psalm must have suggested itself to him as he went forth in the morning to his daily toil, or returned from it at eventide.

John Brown's house is a prominent object,

Appendix.

and the only one in sight, — a simple, plain wooden structure, with a larger barn near by, in which I saw, as I passed by, a fine load of newly made hay. We entered the front door and met Mr. Hinckly, who married one of John Brown's daughters.

He had a very intelligent countenance. He was one the "chosen band" (in Kansas), and had a sincere reverence for his great leader and for the objects he had in hand.

Mr. Hinckly regards Brown as the pioneer — as in fact the first martyr — in this war. I think he is right in his judgment of John Brown's position as history will put him.

I read to my boys and my brother the touching account of Brown's death, in order to impress upon my young companions the real nobleness of the soul whose body's resting place we were going to visit. Eight or ten rods from the door is seen a huge bowlder, rising about ten feet high, rugged and broad, and having a rather grand, irregular shape, making four massive sides. Directly in front of one of these, and facing, or nearly facing, the front door of the residence, lies John Brown, "alone in his glory." A magnificently broad sodded tumulus alone marks the spot. I like its size. It was worthy in this respect to be placed over the remains of one of the old Scandinavian Vikings, huge and simple as his own great nature. It is surrounded by rose-bushes, a little neglected. In front of it, and very awkwardly placed, is a tall, crumbling headstone, given originally to John Brown to mark the grave of his father, of the same name. Below the name of the father and time of his death appears, rudely cut and easily to be effaced, the statement that another John Brown was executed at Charlestown, Va., 1859. On the back of the slab were the names of the family; but it was all sad, as we thought, and my brother William and I almost vowed that we would send up a good stone-cutter, who, after removing the grotesque and inappropriate slab to another part of the lot, should be directed to cut *deeply* into one of the sides of the massive bowlder above mentioned, the simple words "John Brown," in large letters that

Appendix. 203

could be seen at a glance from as great a distance as one could see the rock itself. This could be done, and the family would consent to it.

It only remains for some of us who believe that such a man is worthy of such a memorial to make proper arrangements for so doing.[1]

Respectfully yours,

HENRY I. BOWDITCH.

---

[1] This was accomplished a few years after the above letter was written. Colonel Francis L. Lee and Hon. George S. Hale had the following inscription deeply cut upon the bowlder, so that neither morbid relic-hunting tourists nor the storms of centuries can blot it out: —

JOHN BROWN

1859

UNFRIENDLY CRITICISM OF JOHN BROWN.

AT the time of John Brown's death, now nearly twenty-eight years ago, his praises were celebrated so eloquently by Emerson, Thoreau, Manning, John A. Andrew, Wendell Phillips, and others, and were so well supported by public opinion, that it seemed as if his fame had been set on an enduring basis forever. Victor Hugo and the English anti-slavery people took up the refrain in Europe, and the reverberation of it had not died away on either side of the Atlantic, before the civil war began, and the John Brown song echoed throughout the land. In 1867, Phillips said of Emerson that after all his chief merit lay in the fact that having talked about heroism all his life, when the hero finally came he knew him.

Now, however, as usually happens, we have an ebb tide again. The opposition, who were formerly constrained to silence by public opinion, come forward now to argue their views before a younger generation, in which there dwells a different spirit from that of the war period. Take any man out of his own time, and place him in another, and he will appear to great disadvantage. Imagine Socrates in the age of the Antonines, or Martin Luther as a contemporary of Voltaire. They would appear as violent or meddlesome persons. So if we take John Brown away from the fearful and exciting period of his career, — a period of dark political intrigues and inhuman plots against the liberties of the people, while the first shocks of a gigantic revolution were agitating the most courageous minds, — if we take him out of the element in which he lived, and study him with the peaceful and commonplace life of to-day as a background, his actions may appear monstrous, his character inhuman, his endeavor a failure. That, however, is not the way to study an historical character. We should either place ourselves in sympathy with the conditions of his life, or leave him alone, and interest ourselves in other subjects.

Henry Wilson, in his hastily constructed history of the anti-slavery struggle, led the way by speaking of the Harper's Ferry invasion as a serious injury to the prospects of the Republican party. This is the natural view of a broad-minded but timid politician, one without much historical insight; but it is a point difficult to prove, since the Republican party was never more successful than during the next twelve months. In Wilson's own State, John A. Andrew, who did not hesitate to preside at a meeting called to raise funds for John Brown's family, was nominated for governor with enthusiasm, and easily elected. Next came an article some years since in the "North American Review," supposed to have been written, or perhaps instigated, by a citizen of Kansas who formerly was a leading spirit in the Free-State movement, but afterward was eclipsed by bolder and more enterprising leaders. Having now outlived most of his rivals, he takes advantage of the fact in a way which is creditable neither to his judgment nor intentions. The article does not even pretend to be an *ex parte* statement, but is a direct attack on John Brown's character, and an undervaluation of his public services. Fortunately for the writer, his efforts to do this have small chance of success, and we trust will be forgotten for the sake of his earlier services in the cause of freedom.

Following shortly after the "North American" article, came an essay on John Brown, by a Boston gentleman, read and presented to the Massachusetts Historical Society. This was also a direct attack upon the man. In it he is said to have been described as either a fanatic or a midnight murderer, and guilty of lynching five innocent Missourians at Pottawatomie. Brown may have been a fanatic in the sense that Peter the Hermit and Cromwell were fanatics, not in the sense that Marat and Wilkes Booth were fanatics. In regard to the Pottawatomie executions, nothing probably will ever be known with certainty. Whether Brown was responsible for them or not, the Free-State party certainly were. It appears to have been a case of retaliatory lynch law. A number of Free-State settlers had been murdered by Missourians in a cowardly and brutal manner that would have disgraced highwaymen. The murderers could not be punished by course of law, and in most cases could not be identified. We know in our own time what ruffians have infested the border counties of Missouri, — the James brothers and others. The men who committed these atrocities were indirectly supported by the President of the United States. It is not in the nature of frontier men to endure such things without reprisals; they would not endure them from Indians, nor from any other species of human fiend. The five Missourians who were shot or stabbed on Pottawatomie Creek, may not have committed these atrocities themselves, but they were known to have been members of the lawless bands which were terrorizing the country round about. That they were "innocent and blameless men" is as unlikely and as difficult to prove as Wilson's statement that the Harper's Ferry invasion injured the prospects of the Republican party. It was a horrible affair, and whether justifiable or not, who shall say? To return good for evil

Appendix.

does not work well in all cases; and vicarious atonement is also a Christian doctrine. Among the Free-State men of Kansas at the time there seems to have been a difference of opinion in regard to it; but we have sufficient evidence in Governor Robinson's cordial indorsement of John Brown to the friends of Kansas in the Eastern States some months afterward that it did not injure him with the leaders of the party. Cæsar, whose merciful nature stands out alone among the soldiers of antiquity, once utterly destroyed a tribe of Germans who had invaded Gaul, men, women, and children. In ordinary men, temporary aberrations are usually caused by outside influences, but in the case of a strong, consistent, and determined character, they must be interpreted in some other way. The lives of such men are like problems in algebra,— the known terms give us the solution of the unknown.

Professor von Holst refers to the Pottawatomie matter as a case of somewhat irregular lynch law, and it has occurred to me that the perfect solution of it can be attained only through a careful study of the customs and traditions of Western frontier life. People who live in comfortable city houses, with a policeman within call of the telephone, cannot easily conceive what it is to be alone at night on the wild prairie with wife and children only, unprotected except by one's own rifle, and one's nearest neighbor perhaps something more of a tiger than a human soul. Laws which apply in the former case are of no value in the other, for the excellent reason that they cannot be executed. John Brown was reared in that same frontier life, and was well versed in its criminal code. It is likely that he acted as his father and his friends would have done had a small band of Indians persisted in establishing themselves too near at hand for public security. The situation of that handful of Free-State settlers at Ossawatomie was truly a terrible one.[1] Peaceable themselves and wishing harm to no one, they felt that they were liable to be attacked at any time, either when at work in

[1] See Sanborn's "Life and Letters of John Brown," pp. 259, 281.

their fields or asleep in their beds, by an enemy overwhelming in numbers, their houses burned, their wives insulted, and driven from their claims, fortunate if they escaped with their lives. The Doyles and Shermans were an advanced post of this enemy, spies almost in their camp. Only two courses lay open to them, — either to move away and leave the fruits of their toil to others; or to get the start of their opponents, brush away the Doyles and Shermans, and clear the decks for action. There was no middle course, nor help to be expected from others. Brave men will usually risk their lives to defend their property, and the Anglo-Saxon race does not bear oppression with equanimity. Least of all was John Brown the person to take a backward step in an affair of this kind; he could no more be cuffed with impunity than a Spanish cavalier of the best period. He was deliberate and cool-headed, but there was spirited dynamite inside of him. The two following cases of frontier justice may place this dubious matter in a clearer light. In 1878, a Ute Indian was found dead in the Colorado forest with a bullet-hole in his body. A detachment of the tribe immediately proceeded to the nearest settlement and shot the first white man they met with, sitting on the piazza of his own ranch. There was great indignation in the community at this retaliatory outrage, but I was informed that both state and federal authorities acquiesced in it as the only kind of justice that Indians could obtain. In February, 1880, I attended a trial for murder in Denver. The prisoner was acquitted by the jury, mainly on the ground that the murdered man had some time previously threatened his life, I think with a revolver. A threat of violence in a so slightly regulated community is necessarily considered equal to an overt act, or at least to the preparation for one. To use a classical comparison, the Pottawatomie affair reminds me of Ulysses' and Diomed's midnight expedition against the Trojans.

In his great oration on "The Crime Against Kansas," the 20th of May, 1856, Charles Sumner gave this prophetic warning to the Demo-

Appendix. 213

cratic Senators: "If you madly persevere, Kansas will not be without her William Tell, who will refuse at all hazards to recognize the tyrannical edict, and this will be the beginning of civil war." A few days later the Pottawatomie executions, as Mr. Sanborn calls them, took place, and the subsequent fights of Black Jack and Ossawatomie verified Sumner's prediction. John Brown, however, was in this respect unlike Tell; he did not risk the life of his son, but struck directly at the tyrant. Bismarck thinks that is what Tell ought to have done. European history is filled with like instances of sudden explosions which have preceded political or religious revolutions, popular feeling concentrating itself in a small group of individuals. The Thirty Years' War began in this way, and so did the Hungarian revolution of 1848, a struggle for independence which was greatly applauded in America. The revolt of Germany against Napoleon in 1813 began with collisions between the French troops and the populace in Berlin, similar to the Boston Massacre. That is the mistake which the gentlemen of the Massachusetts Historical Society make now in regard to Crispus Attucks. Their estimate of him is not historical but conventional. Evidently they do not realize in what shape the burning passion of patriotism may develop itself in rude, uncultured natures. Upon what testimony do they denounce him as a "notorious negro spoiling for a fight"? Even if that were the fact, as possibly it may be, it would not necessarily change the character of the act in which he lost his life. Rowdies who are spoiling for a fight do not commonly expose themselves to imminent death, and though an unlettered man, he seems to have shown such a spirit of self-sacrifice as would do honor to any college graduate. Too dull, perhaps, to understand the legal relation between England and her colonies, he looked upon the redcoat soldiers only as instruments of an oppression against which he rebelled with all his might. Upon which side were the sympathies of our Historical Society in 1775, or during the dishonorable presidency of Buchanan, and the crime

Appendix.

against Kansas? It is indeed true that all the members of that society are not, in regard to John Brown at least, of the same mind, and one of its most cultivated and honorable associates has made a vigorous defence there of the old Puritan hero, as I believe he called him. At the John Brown meeting held in November, 1859, and presided over by John A. Andrew, the pastor of the Old South Church, Rev. Mr. Manning, drew a parallel between John Brown and Crispus Attucks, as the white man who was sacrificing himself for the black race, and the black man who had sacrificed himself for the white race. It would not be just to John Brown, however, to carry the comparison beyond an historical similarity, for the relative importance of their acts differ as greatly as the men themselves. Finally, Hay and Nicolay in their "Life of Abraham Lincoln" have given a disparaging account of John Brown which is much more dangerous than any preceding attack upon his life and character.

It is more dangerous, not only because of the large circulation of the book, but also because it is written with what might be called the negative bias of impartiality, as man is unconsciously prejudiced in regard to a certain action, mentally condemns it without proper investigation, and then decides to write an impartial account of it. This I think is what Hay and Nicolay have done in the present instance, and the mischief of it is that it gives their writing the appearance of being dispassionate, when it is not so at all. Their intentions are doubtless good, but they do not apprehend the processes of their own minds. They would do John Brown justice if they saw him clearly as he was; but they do not see him clearly as he was. The case is as if one were to judge a stained-glass window in a mediæval church by its dull and wire-covered exterior. Go within the church and look at it *with the light shining through*, and it becomes a glorious spectacle. John Brown's achievements, looked at from the *outside* would not surpass those of Andreas Hofer; looked at in the light of their spiritual significance, and he becomes the most modern type of a world-hero. It is one of the materialistic tendencies of our time that writers come more and more to consider surfaces only. This is what Mr. Howells means by what he calls realism, and consequently he relegates heroism to the infatuations of the past. Mankind can always be divided into classes; those to whom "the primrose by the river's brim" is a picture of heavenly love and purity, and those to whom it is only a yellow primrose. This may not be democratic, but according to the view of these writers neither is heroism a democratic virtue. Democracy, as its name implies, is a principle of politics, and has no place in ethics or literature.

John Brown, moreover, was a unique character, so different from his cotemporaries that even among his admirers few can be said to have penetrated to the very heart of the man. No one should be blamed for not understanding him, or for misunderstanding him. There are excellent painters who do not appreciate the drawings of Da Vinci, and good composers who cannot realize the superiority of Bach's music. It is not any fault of theirs, but the accident of temperament, education, or mental capacity. What is difficult of comprehension attracts and interests the civilized man; but the pedant despises it, and the barbarian hates it. We should always endeavor to respect what we do not comprehend; for so only can we hope finally to comprehend it.

In Hay and Nicolay's account of Brown, there is a certain kind of disparagement from beginning to end. Everything about him is represented in the hardest, most uncharitable way. He is spoken of as a man generally unsuccessful in a variety of vocations; his services in Kansas are discredited; his presumed connection with the Pottawatomie affair is enlarged upon and presented in an unfavorable light; he is represented as practising deceit on the Kansas aid committees; his invasion of Virginia is criticised from a military point of view, certainly the most inapplicable of all points of view from which to see it; he is described as a man "of unbounded courage and little wisdom; crude, visionary ideality;" of "ambition curbed to irritation; . . . in language and conduct he was clean, but coarse; honest, but rude; ... his courage partook of the recklessness of insanity;" and finally the victor of the Ossawatomie fight is represented as "of military ability too insignificant even for ridicule." Is this one of the results of Mr. Howells's doctrine of realism in writing? Surely nothing could be more unsympathetic.

I will add one short paragraph to show more plainly the temper of this historian: —

"But merely to conceive great enterprises is not to perform them, and every after-step of John Brown reveals his lamentable weakness and utter inadequacy for the heroic rôle to which he fancied himself called. His first blunder was in divulging all his plans to Forbes, an utter stranger, while he was so careful in concealing them from others. Forbes, as ambitious and reckless as himself, of course soon quarrelled with him and left him, and endeavored first to supplant, and then betray him."

As these remarkable statements have, to use a geological expression, all the same "dip," I shall only attempt to reply to one or two of them, which may do for the whole. In regard to John Brown's conduct and language, it was sufficiently refined for him to appear to advantage among the most cultivated men and women of Boston. Never was a man more transparent. His ethical purity, and the innate nobility of his spirit were not written on his face, but shone through it. It was this which always inspired confidence in him among high-minded men, as among vulgar people he was often despised for the very same reason. His handwriting, though somewhat cramped, was in general style much like Abraham Lincoln's; and Emerson, in the deliberative reflection of after years, coupled his address to the court in Virginia with Lincoln's Gettysburg speech as "the most eloquent words of the present century." Mr. Lowell also, I believe, has pronounced Brown's letter in which he describes the incidents and adventures of his early life to be one of the finest pieces of autobiography extant. In style, his writing is plain, sensible, and kind, which are also the distinctive characteristics of Lincoln's speeches.

People who are exclusively non-resistants, and those who know what is at the bottom of

Appendix. 221

the sea, may satisfy themselves that there was no need of fighting in Kansas in 1856, but they will never convince many others. What has been we sometimes know; what might have been who can tell? That the Civil War began in Kansas has become a proverbial expression. If fighting was necessary in one case it was in the other; and there has never been any question but that John Brown did the bravest fighting against the Missouri invaders of Kansas. Colonel Lane is credited with having been a brave man and ready for a fight, but he never had much chance, for Captain Brown was always before him. What would the Free-State settlers have done without Brown and Lane to defend them? I think they would have mostly emigrated to Nebraska, and left Kansas to be filled up with slave-holders. "Courage," Dr. Johnson said, "is the most important of all virtues, for without it the others are of no avail." The books which have been written to prove that the Civil War might have been avoided by a few more concessions to the slavocracy, and that Buchanan's policy toward the rebellious

South was dictated by patriotic motives, are based upon a misunderstanding of human nature, and their writers can have but a weak sense of national honor. John Brown's invasion of Virginia was only the continuation of hostilities, the inevitable change from a successful defence to offensive operations.

The Harper's Ferry attack was not a success from a military point of view, or even from that of guerilla warfare; but to call John Brown an unsuccessful man is to deny history. It is difficult to understand how it could have been otherwise than unsuccessful, but those who have accomplished any great work by their own unaided exertions, and have not been mere flies on the wheel of prosperity, — those know right well the narrow line that divides success from failure. John Brown, like Garibaldi, possessed a genius for irregular warfare, a very rare kind of genius. The methods of such men are a secret which, like that of Titian's coloring, dies with them. How can any of us who are wholly incapable of such great actions pretend to judge them with exactness? Indeed, in a higher sense, as Lin-

Appendix. 223

coln said at Gettysburg, we have no right to judge them. Not to be satisfied with their result would be ungenerous. The ignominy of failure fell at John Brown's feet like broken chains, and the moral grandeur of the man shone forth from the Charlestown jail with such a light that friends and foes bowed their heads in homage, and men of all nations rose to their feet with a shout of applause. It was like a bright meteor crossing the black sky of American politics and disappearing forever. He shook the South as Neptune was fabled to shake the nations with his trident, and Lincoln's army which invaded Virginia twenty months afterward was much less successful and produced less consternation.

"But John Brown was a rebel, and Lincoln the lawfully elected President," say alike the comfortable aristocrat depending on his traditions and the honest democrat holding fast to party principles. So was Henry Tudor a rebel when he fought against Richard III., and William of Orange when he opposed the Spaniard, and so were Washington and Mirabeau rebels. Those men had law and authority pitched against them. They were the champions of a higher law and acted under it. When laws become unendurable, when, as Lowell says, "right is ever on the scaffold, wrong forever on the throne," then rebellion is a virtue and the higher law comes into play. Froude states it exactly when he says, "High treason is either the greatest of crimes or the noblest of virtues;" which it is depends upon the circumstances of the case. Webster wished to know where the higher law was to be found; but when there is no such law in the hearts of men the laws in the statute-books have little force, as is the case in Mexico and portions of South America. On another occasion Webster also might have admitted this, for if he was not a man of keen moral sense, neither was he a narrow legal pedant. There is at least one form of higher law which even the most pedantic lawyers are compelled to recognize, and that is the right of revolution.[1] The de-

[1] There can be no stronger statement of the right of revolution than is to be found in Webster's reply to Colonel Hayne.

Appendix. 225

feated party in a revolution rarely, if ever, justifies it, and the successful party invariably justifies it; but every one is sure to justify *some* revolution. Southerners might condemn the acts of John Brown, but the bombardment of Fort Sumter was just as illegal. Englishmen may think that we separated from the mother country without sufficient cause, but they all justify the glorious revolution of 1688. The French jurists of the restoration were not so unwise as to attempt a return to the legal status of Louis XVI.; and when Charles X. did so he was immediately dethroned. It was the higher law which Jennie Geddes appealed to when she hurled her chair at the Scotch bishop and cried out, " Are you going to say mass in kirk?" It was the higher law which our forefathers appealed to when they declared " No taxation without representation." It was under authority of the higher law that Lincoln issued his proclamation of freedom to the slaves. So far as the practice of law is influenced by legal principles rather than the customs of mankind, and so far as legislators in framing the statutes are influenced by an idea of right and justice, just so far is the higher law recognized and accepted by the legal profession. Truly, it is this ideal of justice which constitutes the higher law.

Hay and Nicolay, however, say that "modern civilization and a republican government require that all coercive reform shall act by authority of law only." This statement is almost worthy of Stephen A. Douglas; for while it seems broad enough to cover the whole question, it contains in substance only a vague and unproven political theory. Great things are to be hoped of republican governments, but the history of our own would show that they are not exempt from tyranny, outrage, and the perversion of right. Read what that most truthful of historians, Dr. H. von Holst, says of the administrations of Jackson, Polk, and Pierce. The United States in 1856, with the noblest statesman of his time struck down at his desk in the Senate, and political murders supported by government authority in Kansas, can hardly be called an instance of modern civilization. The Southern States at that time were in a condition resembling that of Italy two thousand years ago. That they were so was wholly owing to the institution of African slavery. We were a republic in form, but an oligarchy of sixty thousand slave-holders had absolute possession of the central government. The human race, however, is governed not more by laws than it is by sentiment, and it was the sentiment of European civilization, of the civilization of New England, and of the sons of New England in the West, which concentrated itself in John Brown, and drove him to his desperate deed. Consecrated like Metius Curtius he leaped into the fiery gulf.

It has been said that he made the Civil War. No doubt he precipitated it, but that is a different thing from being responsible for it. Frederick the Great precipitated the Seven Years' War; but he did so, as we all know, as an act of self-defence. If any one individual was responsible for the war it was Stephen A. Douglas, with his iniquitous Kansas-Nebraska bill, all the more iniquitous since it pretended to be based on democratic principles. Next to Douglas come Franklin Pierce and Caleb Cushing, with their support of the "law and order party" in Kansas. H. von Holst has made this so plain that only those who are perverse can fail to be convinced of it. In brief, the slavery question might be compared to a powder magazine, covered up and protected by Henry Clay with successive layers of compromise, the last of which included Webster's Fugitive Slave Law. Through all these protections Douglas bored a hole with a sharp auger called the Kansas-Nebraska bill; Pierce then laid the train, which was suddenly exploded by John Brown in a flash of heaven's own lightning.

In a higher sense, as Lincoln would have said, it seems almost a pity that anything should have been written about John Brown. Almost immediately from the time of his death he became an ideal character in the thoughts of men. Probably he will remain so in spite of all that may be said about him; and in some future age, a more poetical and less critical one than the present, it is likely he will become the central figure in some epic commemorating the great anti-slavery struggle. Since Cromwell's time there has been perhaps no other such grand personality. His features, " chiselled as it were in granite," bore the stamp of the hero; and when Brackett's bust of him was placed among those of the Roman emperors in the Athenæum, it made them all to appear insignificant. Wasson said of him, " His was the most determined face I ever beheld. His lips were like the lips of fate, and yet they met together as lightly as rose petals. There was no contraction of the facial muscles, no clinching of the teeth; his determination was of a pure moral quality. Like Socrates, the man was possessed of a genius which was too much for him." The penetrating look of his eye has been already mentioned, but the tone of his voice was also so penetrating that its echoes are sometimes yet to be heard. Two years since I met a South Carolinian who had been a colonel in the Confederate army, and he told me quite a dramatic story of an interview between John Brown and Governor Wise of Virginia, and as he repeated the words, " It is only a brief moment, Governor Wise, that any of us live on this earth," the tones of the narrator's voice startled me, for I heard in them the tone of Brown's own voice again after twenty-five years. Now this colonel had not received this story directly from Governor Wise, but at second or third hand. The oft repeated tale that Governor Wise was profoundly impressed by the bearing and conversation of John Brown has lately received positive confirmation from Gen. S. C. Armstrong of Hampton, Va. Brown, Lincoln, and Sumner seem to be the three Northern men of that time for whom Southerners have the most respect.

One is glad to learn from Sanborn's biography that John Brown's friends endeavored most earnestly to dissuade him from the Virginia expedition. Finally, being unable to move him, they proved themselves true and loyal friends, and gave him all the moral and material support they could. "You see how it is," said Gerrit Smith, " our dear old friend has made up his mind to this course, and cannot be turned from it. We cannot give him up to die alone; we must support him." This loyalty to friends

Appendix. 231

and kindred was the basis of all virtue in the earlier ages of history; and although in modern life a regard for abstract right is held to be superior to it, cases still occur in which amid a conflict of duties we are compelled to fall back again on the old corner-stone of human society. It was in such Homeric sense that his most intimate friends supported John Brown in his attempt to liberate the negroes of the South. Froude says that healthy natures act more from feeling than reflection, and in spite of his intense moral earnestness Brown was a healthy, practical nature, — one that looked facts full in the face, and felt the firm earth always under his feet. His presentiment of accomplishing great things in Virginia was justified by the result, though in a different way from what he had at first anticipated.

When in 1863, George L. Stearns was establishing a bureau for the recruitment of colored troops at Buffalo, he and one of his subordinates happened to be taking dinner one day at a hotel on the Canadian side of Niagara River. At the same table were a number of secessionists who having by chance escaped from the Confederacy were in no hurry to return South again. Having discovered that Mr. Stearns was from Boston, they talked to each other about the cowardly Yankees and "nigger" Abolitionists in such loud tones as were evidently intended to taunt and exasperate him. Having endured this for some time he finally turned to his companion and said in a clear, strong voice, "Mr. ——, I consider it the proudest act of my life that I gave good old John Brown every pike and rifle he carried to Harper's Ferry." Such a retort was more than his tormentors had looked for; they seemed abashed by it and soon left the room. I believe that all of Brown's friends felt that having known him was the highest honor and good-fortune.

THE END.

JOHN BROWN NÉ À TORRINGTON LE 9 MAI 1800.

À LA MÉMOIRE
DE
JOHN BROWN,
ASSASSINÉ JURIDIQUEMENT
À CHARLESTOWN LE 2 DÉCEMBRE
1859,
ET À CELLE DE SES FILS ET DE SES
COMPAGNONS MORTS VICTIMES DE
LEUR DÉVOUEMENT À LA CAUSE
DE LA LIBERTÉ DES
NOIRS.

Yᵉ Bookworme

Yᵉ Olde Colonial Time

Extracts from

Cupples & Hurd's List,

✳︎ 𝔈𝔥𝔢 𝔄𝔩𝔤𝔬𝔫𝔮𝔲𝔦𝔫 𝔓𝔯𝔢𝔰𝔰 ✳︎

Boston.

MESSRS. CUPPLES AND HURD,

Booksellers, Publishers, Printers and Importers, Boston, have constantly on hand a full stock of Standard American and English Publications, including many choice editions, and all books of literary value.

English and all Foreign books received immediately on publication, and imported to order at reasonable rates.

Particular attention given to procuring books which are out of print, and to supplying Public Libraries and other Institutions duty free.

The newest books and magazines are always in stock; all orders by mail receiving prompt attention. Subscriptions received for periodicals in all languages, and special care is given to the binding of books and periodicals in every style.

With **The Algonquin Press** *at their command, they are prepared to execute with judgment every description of printing, from the finest illustrated book to the artistic detail of a circular or an invitation card.*

"Good as it is to inherit a library, it is better to collect one. Each volume then, however lightly a stranger's eye may roam from shelf to shelf, has its own individuality, a history of its own. You remember where you got it, and how much you gave for it. . . . The man who has a library of his own collection is able to contemplate himself objectively, and is justified in believing in his own existence. No other man but he would have made precisely such a combination as his. Had he been in any single respect different from what he is, his library, as it exists, never would have existed. Therefore, surely he may exclaim, as in the gloaming he contemplates the backs of his loved ones, 'They are mine, and I am theirs.'"

Obiter Dicta.

www.ingramcontent.com/pod-product-compliance
Lightning Source LLC
Chambersburg PA
CBHW060150050426
42446CB00013B/2751